ZORBÁ

ZORBÁ

Book by Joseph Stein

Music by John Kander

Lyrics by Fred Ebb

Adapted from Zorbá the Greek *by Nikos Kazantzakis*

Original Broadway Version

RANDOM HOUSE • NEW YORK

ZORBÁ *was first presented by Harold Prince in association with Ruth Mitchell at the Imperial Theatre, New York, New York, on November 17, 1968, with the following cast:*

NIKOS	John Cunningham
ZORBÁ	Herschel Bernardi
HORTENSE	Maria Karnilova
MIMIKO	Al DeSio
WIDOW	Carmen Alvarez
MANOLAKAS	James Luisi
MAVRODANI	Paul Michael
PAVLI	Richard Dmitri
LEADER	Lorraine Serabian
CONSTABLE	David Wilder
PRIEST	Gerard Russak
OLD MAN	Robert Bernard
KATAPOLIS	Richard Nieves
GEORGI	John La Motta
KONSTANDI	Joseph Alfasa
DESPO	Nina Dova
SOFIA	Marsha Tamaroff
EFTERPI	Lee Hooper
MARINA	Alicia Helen Markarian
FIVOS	Gerrit de Beer
BELLY DANCER	Jemela Omar
ATHENA	Peggy Cooper
VASILIS	Martin Meyers
CHYRISTO	Louis Garcia
ALEXIS	Alex Petrides
PANAYOTIS	Nat Horne
KYRIAKOS	Jerry Sappir
KANAKIS	Ali Hafid
KOSTANTINOS	Angelo Saridis

LOUKAS	Loukas Skipitaris
MEROPI	Juliette Durand
ARISTOS	Charles Kalan
ANTONIS	Anthony Marciona
TASSO	Susan Marciona
THANOS	Lewis Gundunas
ALIKI	Miriam Welch
ZACHARIAS	Edward Nolfi
IRINI	Connie Burnett
GRIGORIS	Wayne Boyd

Some of the characters and members of the CHORUS also play the various minor roles of MAN 1, MAN 2, MAN 3, MAN 4, MAN 5, WOMAN 1, WOMAN 2, YOUNG MAN, MAN IN CHORUS, GIRL, WAITER, CAFÉ PROPRIETOR, ADMIRALS AND SEXTON.

Directed by Harold Prince

Choreographed by Ronald Field

Scenic production by Boris Aronson

Lighting by Richard Pilbrow

Costumes by Patricia Zipprodt

Musical direction by Harold Hastings

Dance music arranged by Dorothea Freitag

ZORBÁ *opened in an extensively revised version at the Broadway Theatre on October 16, 1983. It was directed by Michael Cacoyannis. Choreography was by Graciela Daniele; scenic design by David Chapman; costumes designed by Hal George and lighting designed by Marc B. Weiss. The cast was as follows (in order of appearance):*

THE WOMAN	Debbie Shapiro
KONSTANDI, TURKISH DANCER, RUSSIAN ADMIRAL	Frank DeSal
THANASSAI, FRENCH ADMIRAL, MONK	John Mineo
CONSTABLE	Raphael LaManna
ATHENA, CROW	Suzanne Costallos
NIKO	Robert Westenberg
ZORBÁ	Anthony Quinn
DESPO, CROW	Panchali Null
MARIKA, CROW	Angelina Fiordellisi
KATINA	Susan Terry
VASSILAKAS	Chip Cornelius
MARINAKOS, MONK	Peter Marinos
MIMIKO	Aurelio Padron
KATAPOLIS, MONK	Peter Kevoian
YORGO, ITALIAN ADMIRAL	Richard Warren Pugh
SOPHIA, CROW	Pamela Trevisani
MAVRODANI	Charles Karel
PAVLI	Thomas David Scalise
MANOLAKAS	Michael Dantuono
THE WIDOW	Taro Meyer
PRIEST, ENGLISH ADMIRAL	Paul Straney
MADAME HORTENSE	Lila Kedrova
MARSALIAS, MONK	Rob Marshall
ANAGNOSTI	Tim Flavin
MARIA, CAFE WHORE	Karen Giombetti

Synopsis of Scenes

The place: Piraeus, Greece, and the island of Crete.
The time: 1924.

MUSICAL NUMBERS

ACT I

"Life Is"	Leader and Company
"The First Time"	Zorbá
"The Top of the Hill"	Leader and Chorus
"No Boom Boom"	Hortense, Zorbá, Nikos and Admirals
"Vive La Différence"	Admirals and Chorus
"The Butterfly"	Nikos, Leader, Widow and Chorus
"Goodbye, Canavaro"	Hortense and Zorbá
Belly Dance	Belly Dancer
"Grandpapa"	Zorbá, Leader and Chorus
"Only Love"	Hortense
"The Bend of the Road"	Leader and Chorus
"Only Love" (Reprise)	Leader

Instrumental Interlude Soloists	Jerry Sappir, Ali Hafid, Angelo Saridis

ACT II

Bells	Dancers
"Y'assou"	Nikos, Zorbá, Hortense, Leader and Chorus
"Why Can't I Speak?"	Widow and Girl
Mine Celebration	Zorbá and Company
"The Crow"	Leader and Chorus
"Happy Birthday"	Hortense
"I Am Free"	Zorbá
"Life Is" (Reprise)	Leader and Company

ACT ONE

ACT ONE

SCENE 1

The stage is bare, and the background neutral. The whole company is seated in two rows in a semicircle, bouzouki style. There are three standing microphones. Everyone has some sort of instrument and they accompany the CHORUS, *both with the instruments and vocal background.*

MAN 1   So, what should we do now?

MAN 2   Want me to sing? *(To the audience)* Anybody here want me to sing?

CROWD   No! . . . Shut up! . . . Shut your face!

MAN 1   How about a story? Hey, let's tell them a story.

WOMAN 1   What story?

MAN 1   The Zorbá story . . .

WOMAN 2   Zorbá! That's an old story!

MAN 1   Old? Forty-fifty years! Old? Let's tell them the Zorbá story, okay?

CROWD   Yeah! . . . Yes . . . Okay . . . Go on.

MAN 3   What's it about?

MAN 1   What's it about? What's any story about? It's about life.

MAN 2   That's right, you know what life is . . .

MAN 4   *(Sarcastic)*   No, what is life, professor?

MAN 2   Life is an hourglass . . .

MAN 5   Oh, boy!

MAN 2   The minute you're born, the sands start running out.

MAN 4   So what's that? Important news?

MAN 2   It's not news. It's philosophy.

MAN 4   It's garbage, that's what it is!

MAN 2   Why am I talking to you? You're an imbecile, Konstandi. You were born an imbecile and you'll die an imbecile.

MAN 4   Is that what you use your philosophy for? I'll crack your head open and watch your philosophy spill all over the floor.

MAN 1   Sit down, Konstandi. Can't you two talk like people?
         (The company sings "Life Is")

MAN 2
         Life is a glass of rum.

MAN 1
         No!
         Life is a sip of sage.

MAN 5
No!
Life is the taste of raki flowing warmly from the cup.

WOMAN 1
Shut up!
Life is a walnut leaf.

WOMAN 2
No!
Life is an olive tree.

MAN 3
No!
Life is a scented, melon-breasted woman when her
    lips are red and full.

MAN 5
Bull!

MAN 2
Life is a pomegranate orchard and two lovers
    passing by it.

MAN 4
Life is my fist in your face if you don't keep quiet!

MAN 2
What did you say?

MAN 4
I said, life is my fist in your face if you don't keep
quiet!

MAN 2
Oh?

MAN 4
>   Oh!
>   *(There is a general rhubarb. The two men approach
>   each other, about to start a fight. The* LEADER *of the*
>   CHORUS *rises. She raises her arms. They all fall
>   quiet)*

LEADER   Wait!

MAN 4   Oh, boy! Are you lucky!

LEADER   Wait! I will tell you. Listen . . . *(She moves to
the center of the stage. They all sit watching her as she
sings)*
>   Life is what you do while you're waiting to die.
>   Life is how the time goes by . . .
>
>   Life is where you wait while you're waiting to leave.
>   Life is where you grin and grieve . . .
>
>   Having if you're lucky,
>   Wanting if you're not;
>   Looking for the ruby
>   Underneath the rot;
>   Hungry for the pilaf
>   In someone else's pot.
>   But that's the only choice you've got!
>   *(There are sounds of agreement from the* CHORUS*)*
>   Life is where you stand just before you are flat.
>   Life is only that, mister,
>   Life is simply that, mister,
>   That and nothing more than that!

CHORUS
>   Life is what you feel.

LEADER AND TWO WOMEN
Life is what you feel.

CHORUS
Till you can't feel at all.

LEADER AND TWO WOMEN
Till you can't feel at all.

LEADER AND CHORUS
Life is where you fly and fall . . .

LEADER
Running for the shelter,
Naked in the snow;
Learning that a tear drops
Anywhere you go;
Finding it's the mud
That makes the roses grow.
But that's the only choice you know!
(The music builds. Now they all rise and dance. The dance grows more and more intense until once more the LEADER *raises her arms. The* CHORUS *sits, facing the audience)*
Wait! Wait! Once again!
(It is very quiet)
Life is what you do while you're waiting to die.
This is how the time goes by . . .

Blackout

SCENE 2

The lights go on as the company is setting up tables, chairs and other props to indicate a waterfront café in Piraeus. During the following dialogue, people seat themselves at the tables. NIKOS *carries an overcoat, a valise and a carton of books to a table and sits there alone. He is in his thirties and is an intellectual, basically a city man, uncomfortable with strange people and in strange places.*

MAN 1   Waiter, waiter, get me a glass of rum.

WAITER   Right away . . .

MAN 2   And two raki here.

WAITER   Just a minute, I'm all alone here.

WOMAN 1   Excuse me, what time does the boat for Crete leave?

WAITER   Soon.

MAN 1   If the captain isn't drunk.

WAITER *(To* NIKOS)   You want something?

NIKOS   Yes. A glass of wine. Sage, I think.

MAN 1   Waiter, when do I get my rum?

WAITER   In a minute. *(To the* WOMAN)   You want something to drink?

WOMAN 1 No, thank you.

WAITER Then you'll have to sit there. On the bench.
(She goes to the bench and sits. ZORBÁ *enters, carrying a knapsack. He is a rugged, lusty man in his mid-sixties, proud and sure of himself)*

MAN 1 *(To* ZORBÁ*)* How does it look out there?

ZORBÁ Choppy. The sea is full of sheep. *(Spots* NIKOS *and goes to him)* Those books . . . this luggage . . . it's yours, no?

NIKOS *(A little surprised)* Yes . . . Why?

ZORBÁ Traveling? Where to?

NIKOS I'm going to Crete. Why do you ask?

ZORBÁ Taking me with you?

NIKOS *(Intrigued)* I don't understand. Do you know me?

ZORBÁ Not yet. But I would like to—why not? I have nothing against you.

NIKOS And you approach a complete stranger and say, "Take me with you." I don't understand.

ZORBÁ *(Exasperated)* I don't understand! I don't understand! We are strangers because we don't know each other. If I go with you, we will know each other and we will stop being strangers.

NIKOS *(Amused)* That makes a crazy kind of logic, I suppose, but—

ZORBÁ   Logic! You know what logic is? Logic is a woman's backside. Ask me to sit down. It's not good for one man to look up to another man.

NIKOS   Sit down.

ZORBÁ   Thanks for asking.
   (He sits)

NIKOS   Tell me, what kind of work do you do?

ZORBÁ   All kinds. With feet, hands, head . . . *(The WAITER passes)* Waiter, two rums. *(To NIKOS)* You were going to ask me to have a drink with you?

NIKOS   If you say so.

ZORBÁ   Thanks for asking.

NIKOS   You say you do all kinds of work. Can you—

ZORBÁ   Yes.

NIKOS   I haven't asked you what yet.

ZORBÁ   Not necessary. I told you I do all kinds of work. Anything I know how to do, I do perfect. Anything I don't know how to do, I do very good. Where are you coming from?

NIKOS   Well, I've just been in Berlin. And before that, Budapest. Not simple, peaceful places, I think. And before that, Athens. I left here three years ago . . . in 1921 . . . the end of '21.

ZORBÁ   And now you're going to Crete. Why Crete?

NIKOS   Well, there's an old abandoned mine there. It belonged to a relative.

ZORBÁ *(Exclaims)*   A mine! I worked as a miner. That I do perfect! Why do you need so many books?

NIKOS   For pleasure . . . for work.

ZORBÁ   For work?

NIKOS   I was a teacher at the university of Athens.

ZORBÁ   A teacher? And now you want to make your fortune from an old mine. That's not easy. When a mine is abandoned, it's not filled to the brim with money.

NIKOS   I know that, but that's not my only reason for going.

ZORBÁ   No? You got a woman there?

NIKOS   There are other reasons for going places.

ZORBÁ *(Considers)*   It's possible. For instance?

NIKOS   Well, sometimes you go someplace to get away from someplace else.

ZORBÁ   Aha, you're running away from a woman!

NIKOS   There are other things in this world besides women.

ZORBÁ   But not so important.

NIKOS   Maybe not.

ZORBÁ Maybe? My friend, there are only two things that make a man a man. What's in his heart and what's in his pants.

NIKOS And what's in his head?

ZORBÁ Comes straight from the heart and the pants.

NIKOS Are you married?

ZORBÁ Me? Am I not a man? I mean blind. I had a wife, four children, a mother-in-law who talked . . . the full catastrophe!

NIKOS Where's your family now?

ZORBÁ Who knows? Where I left them. The children are grown, all but one. And he's dead.

NIKOS I'm sorry. How old was he?

ZORBÁ Why are you asking? You don't care. *(A pause)* Too young to die! Too damn young to die! *(Recovers)* And you, married?

NIKOS No. I've never been married.

ZORBÁ *(Admiringly)* Never married—maybe those books do make you smart. *(Picks up the parcel of books tied together with a rope)* Lenin. Plato. Buddha, eh! *(Tosses the books aside)* Well, what do you say? Are you taking me with you?

NIKOS Well . . .

ZORBÁ *(Annoyed)* You carry a pair of scales in your head, don't you? You weigh everything to the nearest gram. I know your trouble. You want to know what I think?

NIKOS Not especially.

ZORBÁ I'll tell you. You think too much. I believe in grabbing at life. Every minute is a new minute. Every second a new second. It never happened before. *(Drinks the liquor)* Here—this liquor. I never tasted anything so good. *(Points to a man)* That face . . . Ever see such a face? Smile. *(The man smiles)* I love that face! And that one . . . *(Points to another, hesitates)* Not so good! But different! *(He sings "The First Time")*
   I hear a bouzouki;
   You can't imagine how often I've heard a bouzouki.
   But each time is the first time!

   I sniff at a woman;
   You can't imagine how often I've sniffed at a woman.
   But each time is the first time!

   I pound on a table.
   I leap on a chair.
   I crawl up a mountain to breathe in the air,
   By now I've stopped counting
   How often I've been there.
   But each time is the first time . . .
   I look at a flower;
   I stick my nose in, or stare at, or sleep on a flower.
   But each time is the first time!

   I soar like a sea gull.
   I stamp like a bull.
   I comb out my whiskers so ladies can pull.
   I chew on the mutton
   Until my belly's full.

But each time . . .
A hat, a dumbek, a person . . . each time is new. Like
for instance, I came up and talked to you. Look how
interesting I am.

NIKOS *(Amused)* That's true . . .

ZORBÁ Even if it's not a long talk. Even if you don't talk
the same language . . . Do you want to hear a story?

NIKOS Well, I . . .

ZORBÁ Then I'll tell you . . . *(He sings)*
There was a night in Beirut, I never will forget,
When I ran across the nicest man I think I ever met.
We were sitting drinking vodka in this waterfront
café.
I could tell he was a Turk, but I liked him anyway.

Well, we had so much to drink that we decided we
should speak,
But I'm not so good in Turkish, he was even worse
in Greek.
Still we wanted to communicate and suddenly by
chance
We hit upon a system and we both began to dance.
We couldn't talk the language so we danced it all
instead,
And the two of us could understand what one another
said.
And we had our conversation, which was crazy, I
recall,
But it seemed it was the first time I had ever talked
at all!
(He motions to a member of the CHORUS*)*
Wait! You!

YOUNG MAN Me?

ZORBÁ Show! *(A young man rises from the* CHORUS. *He is now playing the part of* ZORBÁ's *Turk. The music plays softly as the Turk dances a few steps)* He says he's from Ankara. *(The Turk dances again)* He says he has a wife and two small children. *(The Turk dances again)* Oh, he says he misses them very much. *(The Turk dances again)* Ah, you see, he has been away now for eighteen months.

MAN IN CHORUS No! Seventeen!

ZORBÁ *(Annoyed. To the Turk)* Say that again! *(The Turk dances the last section again.* ZORBÁ *stands corrected)* Seventeen! *(He sings)*
> I walk with the devil, he gives me a poke,
> And all ten commandments go right up in smoke.
> But each one I've broken, I feel that I broke
> For the first time,
> The first time.
>
> I talk to a stranger;
> You can't imagine how often I've talked to a stranger.
> But each time . . .
> This time . . .
> Is the first time!
> Well, do we drink to us . . . boss?

NIKOS *(A moment's hesitation)* We drink to us! (ZORBÁ *smacks him on the back. They drink)* I'm happy to have you with me. May God also be with us.

ZORBÁ *(Calmly)* God and the devil.

NIKOS The devil?

ZORBÁ   They travel together, boss. Always together . . .
   (Lifts the valise. Indicates the books) I'll take them.
      (They start to exit)

NIKOS   You haven't told me your name.

ZORBÁ   Zorbá. My name is Zorbá.
      (They exit)

Blackout

Scene 3

The time is late morning. The scene is the exterior of a village café in Crete. The café is on the village square; several small shops as well as the steps and entrance to the village church are visible. Some men are sitting at tables outside the café, drinking; some are playing backgammon or dominoes. Among them are MAVRODANI, *a stern, hard man, about fifty, and his younger brother* MANOLAKAS, *equally stern, equally hard. The village* CONSTABLE *is watching a domino game. From time to time, a* WOMAN *enters from a shop or into a shop. Someone is idly playing an instrument, and at moments during the scene one or another of the villagers reacts to the music with a brief, spontaneous burst of dancing or rhythmic handclapping.*

GEORGI *(A villager. To the* CONSTABLE*)*   When did he say he was coming?

CONSTABLE *(Absorbed in the game)*   What?

GEORGI   The new owner, what time did he say he was coming?

CONSTABLE   He didn't say.

GEORGI   But you said today? Are you sure he's coming today?

CONSTABLE   That's what he wrote. Today.

KATAPOLIS *(A villager)*   But who knows if he's going to start the mine again. Did he say he was going to start the mine again?

CONSTABLE *(Irritated)*   Here's his letter. Read it yourself. *(Hands him the letter)* Stop bothering me.

MANOLAKAS   We could use the work here. The devil has cursed the crops this year.

MARINA *(A villager)*   Quiet, don't talk about the devil. He may hear you.

KATAPOLIS   He's been here already. Look at the fields. *(A boat horn is heard as MIMIKO enters. He is a timid, simple-minded boy, about nineteen, "the village fool")*

MIMIKO *(Excited)*   The boat . . . it's coming in. The big boat is coming! *(No one pays any attention to him. He rushes off)*

CAFÉ PROPRIETOR *(To the CONSTABLE)*   It is understood, of course, that the new owner will stay at my place, above the café . . .

OLD MAN   Why your place? I have an empty house, plenty of room.

CAFÉ PROPRIETOR   Who will cook for him? You? I have a wife.

OLD MAN   I can cook, I can cook . . . *(Appeals to the CONSTABLE)* Lukas, why not my place?

CONSTABLE   It's not for me to say, uncle. Wait till he gets here.

(PALVI *enters. He is a forlorn, clumsy, pathetic man in his twenties; his attitude is weak and hangdog*)

MAVRODANI *(Sharply)*   Where have you been, Pavli?

PAVLI   No place, papa.

MAVRODANI   Waiting outside the widow's house again? Did she chase you again? *(He doesn't answer)* Answer me!

GEORGI *(Taunting)*   Did you catch a glimpse of her this time, Pavli?

MAVRODANI   Why her? There are other women here. Why her? And no one else. Has she cast a spell on you?

PAVLI   I don't know. I want her. Papa, maybe you could talk to her for me.
      (The men laugh. Even PAVLI *smirks)*

DESPO *(A villager)*   Laugh, laugh! Today it's Pavli, tomorrow it will be another. She is evil, that one!

MAVRODANI *(To* PAVLI*)*   Stay away from her, do you hear me?

MANOLAKAS   You are shaming us, Pavli. You are shaming our family.

PAVLI *(Cries)*   Leave me alone, leave me alone . . .

KONSTANDI *(A villager. Looks off, taunting)*   Hey, Pavli, maybe *she* followed *you* this time . . . It's the she-devil herself.
      (The WIDOW *enters. She is a beautiful woman in*

her late twenties, silent and somber. There is an air of tragedy about her)

GEORGI   Widow, isn't that bed of yours cold these nights? I'll warm it up for you.
(She disregards him)

KATAPOLIS *(As she passes, he grabs at her)* What a shame . . . to let this soft body go to waste . . .

MAVRODANI *(Stops her)* You! Why do you turn your face from my son? Are you too good for him? Are you too good for anyone? Widow?
(The WIDOW stares at him and walks by him. PAVLI suddenly rushes up to her)

PAVLI   Let me go home with you . . . I beg you . . .

WIDOW *(Contemptuously)* Go away . . . and wipe your nose!
(She brushes past him and exits. The men laugh at him)

KATAPOLIS   You're not big enough for her, Pavli. She needs a real man.
(MAVRODANI goes over to PAVLI and slaps him sharply. PAVLI rushes off)

OLD MAN   Poor Pavli. She'll never have him. *(The men laugh)* Laugh! You've chased after her, you've grabbed at her. I've seen it myself.

MANOLAKAS   That's enough, granddad!
(He exits as MIMIKO runs back on)

MIMIKO   He's coming! He's coming! It's him!

CONSTABLE *(Looks off)* There are two of them.
(After a moment, ZORBÁ *and* NIKOS *enter, both of them laden down with luggage and parcels. As they put their burdens down, the* CONSTABLE *steps forward)*

CONSTABLE It's a great honor to welcome you to our village, sir! You are the new owner of the mine?

NIKOS That's right.

CONSTABLE I am the constable here. I received your letter. Welcome!

NIKOS Thank you.

KATAPOLIS Are you going to start the mine again? Will there be work?

ZORBÁ There will be work. Anyone who wants to work, report to the mine early tomorrow morning. This here is the boss. He knows nothing about mines; I'm in charge.

NIKOS Now, Zorbá, just a minute.

ZORBÁ What's the difference if I tell them now, boss. They're going to find it out soon enough.

NIKOS *(Amused)* But you could have put it more delicately.

ZORBÁ Maybe you're right, boss. *(To the villagers)* Listen, even if he doesn't know anything, he's still the boss. *(To* NIKOS) Is that better?

NIKOS *(Amused)* It will have to do . . .
     (A PRIEST *steps forward)*

PRIEST I am Father Zahoria and I, too, wish to welcome
you to our village.

ZORBÁ *(Aside to* NIKOS) Watch it, boss.

PRIEST We would be happy if you could attend services
at our church.

NIKOS Thank you, Father, but I must admit I am not a
regular churchgoer.
     (The PRIEST *looks at* ZORBÁ)

ZORBÁ And I am a regular no-churchgoer. No offense,
Father.

PRIEST I hope you will both find the time to come. An
opening of the mine could be most helpful to our village. I will be happy to bless your work.

NIKOS Thank you, Father, and I will be glad to make a
contribution to your church.

PRIEST *(Disregards* ZORBÁ. *To* NIKOS) You're very kind.
Thank you. God be with you.
     (He exits)

NIKOS *(Turns to the* CONSTABLE) Where can we find a
place to live?

CAFÉ PROPRIETOR I have a nice room right over the
café.

NIKOS One room?

CAFÉ PROPRIETOR Well, maybe he will sleep with my two sons . . . *(He indicates* ZORBÁ*)*

ZORBÁ I don't sleep with sons!

OLD MAN *(Interrupts)* I can take them. I have no children, plenty of room.

CAFÉ PROPRIETOR Too late, uncle. I spoke first.

NIKOS We would like to stay together. We'll go to your place.
          (He indicates the OLD MAN*)*

OLD MAN Good. Wonderful. I won't charge too much . . . Come this way. *(The* OLD MAN *picks up the books.* NIKOS *and* ZORBÁ *pick up the bags . . . The village street closes before them as they start off,* MIMIKO *following them)* I will cook for you. It will be extra, of course. I will clean up, too. That's extra.

ZORBÁ I'll do the cooking.

OLD MAN No, cooking comes with the room. And food. All extra.

ZORBÁ I'll cook.

OLD MAN I'll cook and wash your clothes. That's extra.

MIMIKO Mr. Boss! Mr. Boss! Madame Hortense . . . up the hill . . . she has rooms . . .

NIKOS What?

MIMIKO The Frenchwoman. She has rooms.

ZORBÁ *(Appealing)* A Frenchwoman! Oh, boss!

OLD MAN Forget about the Frenchwoman. It's way up the hill, a hard walk . . .

NIKOS Well, since my friend wants to do the cooking, and you have all those extras, we'll try the French-woman.

ZORBÁ *(Slaps* NIKOS *on the back)* Bravo, boss. More and more I know you, more and more I like you.

OLD MAN But you promised me . . .

ZORBÁ We're going to the Frenchwoman . . . and shut up!

OLD MAN *(Taken aback)* Why "shut up"?

ZORBÁ That's extra! *(Picks up the luggage. To* MIMIKO*)* Which way?

MIMIKO This way!
(As they start to pick up the luggage and leave, the CHORUS *appears, beckoning them. The* LEADER *and two men in the* CHORUS *lead off in singing "The Top of the Hill")*

TRIO
Zorbá! Zorbá! Zorbá! Zorbá!
There's a house at the top of the hill where
    someone's waiting for you,
Waiting for you!

There's a room in a house at the top of the hill
    where someone's waiting for you,
Waiting for you!

There's a door to the room in a house at the top
        of the hill where someone's waiting for you,
Waiting for you!

LEADER
There's a woman at the door.

MAN 1
There's a woman at the door.

MAN 2
There's a woman at the door

TRIO
To the room in a house at the top of the hill
Waiting for you!

MAN 1
And the roof is red.

LEADER
And the woman is French.

MAN 2
And the walls are white.

LEADER
And the woman is French.

MAN 1
And the steps run down.

LEADER
And the woman is French.

MAN 2
And the well is cool.

LEADER

And the woman is French

TRIO

At the house at the top of the hill,
Zorbá!

MAN 3

And the ouzo's weak.

LEADER

And the veal is tough.

WOMAN 1

And the bed is hard.

LEADER

And the sheet is rough.

MAN 4

And the bread is old.

LEADER

And the wine is hot.

MAN 3

And the nights are cold

LEADER

But the woman is not,

ALL

At the house at the top of the hill.

The night is cold but the woman is not,
    in the house at the top of the hill

There's a house at the top of the hill where
    someone's waiting for you,
Waiting for you!

There's a room in a house at the top of the hill
    where someone's waiting for you,
Waiting for you!

There's a door to the room in a house at the top of
    the hill where someone's waiting for you,
Waiting for you.

There's a woman at the door.
There's a woman at the door.
There's a woman at the door.
    *(At the conclusion of the song, the hill setting
    opens, revealing the garden of* HORTENSE'S *inn.*
    MIMIKO *runs on, carrying his bundle)*

MIMIKO *(Calls)* Madame . . . Madame Hortense . . .
Madame, people are coming.

HORTENSE *(From behind the house)* Who?

MIMIKO Men. Two of them.

HORTENSE *(Excited, nervous)* Two men? Here? When?

MIMIKO Right now. Coming up the hill.

HORTENSE Oh. Oh, my. Oh, my goodness.

TRIO
    Zorbá! Zorbá!
    There's a house at the top of the hill

Where someone's waiting for you,
Waiting for you,
Waiting for you . . .
*(The song ends as the next scene begins, with no
break in the action)*

SCENE 4

The garden of HORTENSE'S *inn is rather shabby, not well cared for. A vine-covered fence and the entrance to the inn are in the background. A section of a small cottage can be seen at the left. There are a small wooden table and a small bench next to the fence.* HORTENSE *enters from the house, acting very coy, as* NIKOS *and* ZORBÁ *appear. She is in her fifties, a faded coquette who still clings to the flirtatious ways of her youth. She wears an old velvet dress, a flower in her bodice and a ribbon in her hair.*

HORTENSE *(Overly gracious)* Welcome, gentlemen! Welcome to my simple establishment!

NIKOS *(Most gracious)* Madame Hortense, I believe? *(She nods politely)* Delighted to meet you, Madame Hortense.
    (He kisses her hand)

HORTENSE *(Very pleased)* Thank you.

ZORBÁ   I, too, am happy to make your acquaintance.
    (He takes her other hand and kisses it heartily)

HORTENSE   Oh, how gallant!

NIKO   We require two beds, Madame Hortense, in separate rooms, if that is possible.

HORTENSE   That small cottage there . . . *(She points to it)* might suit you. And it's very reasonable.

NIKOS *(Starts toward it)*   This one here?

ZORBÁ   It's all right, boss; it looks perfect. Don't it.

NIKOS *(A little annoyed at him. To* HORTENSE*)*   I'm sure it will suit us splendidly.

HORTENSE   Wonderful. (MIMIKO *enters from the house with a tray, a bottle of wine and two glasses)* I thought a drop of wine might refresh you after your journey . . .

ZORBÁ *(Indicating* HORTENSE*)*   What did I tell you, boss —*this* is what I call an extra!

HORTENSE *(Aside to* MIMIKO, *indicating the luggage)* Bring those into the cottage, Mimiko.
(He picks them up and starts off)

NIKOS   Very thoughtful of you, Madame Hortense.
*(*ZORBÁ *has surreptitiously hidden one glass)*

ZORBÁ   But . . . only one glass?

HORTENSE *(Flustered)*   I put two on the tray, I'm sure I put two on the tray. *(She looks around distractedly)* I suppose it's your coming so unexpectedly . . . Excuse me, I'll get another glass.
(She exits, tripping as she goes out, then smiling back at them)

ZORBÁ *(Moves the bench toward the table, delighted)* Oh, boss, did you see the way that ancient siren swings her hips. . . . Take it from me, boss: it's the old birds make the best stew.

NIKOS   But you just met the lady. How do you know she even likes you?

ZORBÁ *(Raises himself to his full height and combs his mustache)*   Why should she be an exception?

NIKOS *(Amused)*   I guess that's true. You are irresistible!
  (HORTENSE *re-enters with a glass)*

HORTENSE   Here we are. Shall I pour?

ZORBÁ *(Gallantly produces the third glass)*   Won't you join us, Madame?

HORTENSE *(Chuckles)*   You played a joke. Isn't that nice? No one has played such a nice joke on me for such a long time . . .

NIKOS   We insist you join us.

HORTENSE *(With coy modesty)*   But I am merely the inn-keeper.

ZORBÁ   Nonsense. Have a drink, Madame. I love to see a lady drink.
  (He pours the wine)

HORTENSE   This feels like a holiday.

ZORBÁ   Wherever you are, dear lady, it is a holiday.
  (He puts his hand on her leg)

HORTENSE *(Smacks him coyly)*   Aren't you an old rip!

ZORBÁ *(Smacks her back playfully)*   I am, Madame, I am!

NIKOS *(Lifts his glass in a toast)*   We will drink to you, Madame Hortense.

ZORBÁ   Boss, with all your books, you can do better than
that.

NIKOS   You're right, of course. *(Lifts his glass again)* Madame Hortense, I didn't expect to find such elegance,
such grace, such courtesy, such beauty in this wild
place. To you!

ZORBÁ   Bravo, now that's a toast!
(They drink)

HORTENSE *(Delighted)*   This reminds me of the old days.

ZORBÁ *(Warmly)*   Ah, the old days . . . *(A brief pause)*
What old days?
(He pours another drink for HORTENSE *and him-
self)*

NIKOS   Yes, I'm curious. What quirk of fate cast such a
delicate creature on these savage rocks?

HORTENSE   Well, I wasn't always as you see me now . . .

ZORBÁ *(Puts his arm around her)*   And what's wrong
with how you are now? Perfect!

HORTENSE *(Chuckling, good-naturedly)*   Hands off, if
you please!

NIKOS   You were saying . . . ?

HORTENSE   I was once a famous artist . . . not a cheap
tavern singer, mind you, a cabaret star, a chanteuse. I
wore silk underclothes with real lace . . .

ZORBÁ   Ah, to have seen you then . . .
(His arm is around her)

HORTENSE *(Sweetly)*   You are very bold.

ZORBÁ   I am a man, my sweet!
   *(He kisses her on the cheek and pours her some
   more wine, which she drinks. She is enjoying herself immensely)*

NIKOS   You were saying . . . ?

HORTENSE *(Bewildered)*   What? *(Then remembers)* I had
an arrangement with a certain admiral . . .

NIKOS   I understand.

HORTENSE *(Coyly. To* NIKOS)   Of course, you do. Crete
was in a state of revolution, and the fleets of four great
powers anchored here. So I also anchored here. Four
great powers, four admirals . . . Ah, you should have
seen them . . .
   (The four ADMIRALS *have appeared at the side of
   the stage, observing the scene.* HORTENSE, ZORBÁ,
   NIKOS *and the* ADMIRALS *sing "No Boom Boom")*

HORTENSE
   There they were, my admirals,
   The image of romance,
   From England, Russia, Italy and France.

   There they were, my brave quartet,
   Dressed in their navy blues
   With wide, plumed hats and golden braid and
      patent-leather shoes.

   They were just about to fire on Crete
   When on my knees, in a pink chemise,
   I distracted them, *toute suite*, by saying . . .

Please sir, little admiral, no boom boom.
Please sir, pretty admiral, no boom boom.

This evening when it's dark,
I'll let you come to my room.
But first you have to promise, no boom boom.

ADMIRALS
Please sir, little admiral, no boom boom.
Please sir, pretty admiral, no boom boom.

AN ADMIRAL
This evening when it's dark,
I'd like to come to your room.

HORTENSE
But first you have to promise,

HORTENSE AND ADMIRALS
No boom boom!

HORTENSE   And they listened to me . . . We could see
the Cretans through the binoculars and they looked so
tiny. And I seized the beard of the Italian admiral—I
was more familiar with him. I seized his beard and said,
"My Canavaro, don't shoot them, don't shoot the little
people." . . . How nice he smelled . . . how nice they
all smelled. *(She sings)*
My Frenchman smelled of lemon,
My Italian . . . violet.
My English smelled of something I forget.

My Russian wore a musk
They make from oily Georgian bark.
I learned each smell
So I could tell
Between them in the dark!

They'd fill a bath with pink champagne,
Then throw me in the tub,
While two would drink, the other two would scrub.
We played that way
Until the day
They set this island free.

And so, my dear,
If Crete's still here,
It's all because of me.

It was I who kept the navy in tow,
But did your king ever say a thing?
Or decorate me? No!
    (She cries)

ZORBÁ
    Please sir, little admiral, no boom boom.

HORTENSE *(Brightening)*
    That's what I always used to say.

ZORBÁ AND NIKOS
    Please sir, pretty admiral, no boom boom.

HORTENSE
    I had a most convincing way.

ZORBÁ AND NIKOS
    This evening when it's dark,
    I'll let you come to my room.

HORTENSE
    But first you have to promise,
    No boom boom.

ZORBÁ
No boom boom.

NIKOS
No boom boom, Madame Hortense.
(Carried away by the excitement, she goes into a dance)

ADMIRALS
Please sir, little admiral, no boom boom.
Please sir, pretty admiral, no boom boom.

This evening when it's dark,
I'll let you come to my room.

ZORBÁ
But first you have to promise,

HORTENSE
Promise, promise, promise,

ZORBÁ, NIKOS AND HORTENSE
No boom boom.
No boom boom.

ALL
No boom boom boom!

HORTENSE   Then the bad days came. My four admirals
had to leave . . . But as they left, they fired off their
guns . . .

ADMIRALS *(Solemnly)*
Boom . . . boom!

HORTENSE
In my honor, they fired off their guns . . .

ZORBÁ *(Gently)*   Boom boom. Boom boom for you.

HORTENSE *(Far away)*   Yes. Boom boom for me.

ZORBÁ *(Rapturously)*   My bouboulina, shut your eyes
. . . shut your eyes, my treasure. I am your Canavaro.

HORTENSE *(Gently)*   Are you?

ZORBÁ   Yes, I am your admiral, my lily white dove. *(She
puts her arm about his neck. He lifts her, and she leans
on his shoulder. He starts into the house, then turns to
NIKOS apologetically)* Excuse us, boss . . . she's in the
mood!
    *(NIKOS looks after them, smiles, lifts his glass and
    toasts)*

NIKOS   To Zorbá and his bouboulina . . . You have my
best wishes and my envy! May your love be as sweet and
as true as this wine . . . And may it last a little longer!
    *(He exits to his cottage. While the scene changes,
    the ADMIRALS and the CHORUS sing, in front of the
    set, "Vive la Différence")*

ADMIRALS AND CHORUS
    Tant qu'il y a une femme,
    Tant qu'il y a un homme,
    Elle est heureuse.
    Vive la différence.

    Tant qu'il y a une robe
    Suivie par une cane,
    Elle est heureuse.
    Vive la différence.

    Vive la différence!
    Cette magique dans l'air—

J'aime la différence;
C'est ça qui fait tourner la terre.

Tant qu'il y a une jupe,
Un coquin dans le coin,
Elle est heureuse.
Vive la différence!
    (The lights dim as the melody is continued on an
    old horned phonograph)

SCENE 5

The stage gradually lights up, revealing HORTENSE'S *bedroom. It is furnished in a flamboyant French style, with artificial flowers, purple cushions, long-legged dolls on the bed, etc.* HORTENSE *and* ZORBÁ *are seen dancing to the music coming from a tiny record on the phonograph.*

HORTENSE *(Coquettish)* You dance strong, like a man should.

ZORBÁ I do everything like a man should.
   (He tries to kiss her)

HORTENSE *(Turns away)* No.

ZORBÁ *(Turns her back)* Yes.

HORTENSE No.

ZORBÁ Yes.

HORTENSE *(Flirty)* Well . . . a little one. (ZORBÁ *kisses her long and lusty. She responds. As he releases her)* What did you say your name was?

ZORBÁ Zorbá. I am Zorbá. But if you like, you can call me Canavaro.
   (They resume dancing . . . The record gets stuck, repeating a phrase. HORTENSE *leaves him and adjusts the record)*

HORTENSE *(Reminiscing)* Canavaro, Canavaro . . .
How young I was then . . . how beautiful I was . . .
how graceful . . . how like a dove I was then.
*(She attempts a pirouette, a suggestion of her
youthful grace)*

ZORBÁ You are beautiful still, my bouboulina, my dove.
And young—you shall be young again.

HORTENSE *(Sadly)* Never.

ZORBÁ And why not? I have a wish for you: may God see
that this year you grow a new clear skin, new straw-
berry hair and, where necessary, new teeth! And may
you rise from the waves once more, my siren, singing
your lovely song. And may the fleets break to pieces on
these two round, magic rocks.
(And he seizes her two breasts)

HORTENSE *(Doesn't pull away)* You're sweet.

ZORBÁ *(Holding her breasts)* And you're . . . juicy!
Juicy as a woman should be . . .
(The record runs down and whines to a stop)

HORTENSE I'm sorry . . . *(Goes to the phonograph and
winds it; the music starts again.* ZORBÁ *curses under his
breath)* You said I shall be young again. How shall I be
young again?

ZORBÁ And why not? Listen, let me tell you about a fine
present I'm going to get you. There's this new doctor, a
Russian, who performs miracles, they say. He gives you
a medicine of some kind—drops or powder—and you
become twenty again . . . twenty-five at most. I'll
have some sent for you.

HORTENSE   If it's drops, you must get me a gallon. And if it's powder—

ZORBÁ   A sackful!

HORTENSE   Ah, to be young again . . . *(She dances by herself, singing. He keeps time, clapping. She stops abruptly)* Oh, I'm dizzy.

ZORBÁ *(Leads her to the bed)*   Here. Lie down, here.

HORTENSE *(Coyly)*   I'll sit.

ZORBÁ   No, lie down. When you're tired or dizzy, it's true that sitting is better than standing. But lying is better than sitting. It is a law of nature.

HORTENSE   You've just made it up.

ZORBÁ   I know, but it's true. Rest here, my sweet, my swan . . . *(She lies down. He sits beside her and . . . the record gets stuck. She starts to rise. Gently)* Please, I'll take care of it . . .
   (He takes the record off and breaks it)

HORTENSE *(Sadly)*   But it's my favorite . . .

ZORBÁ   I'll buy you another one, a new one . . . *(Goes to her)* Please, don't disturb yourself, my virgin . . .

HORTENSE *(Startled)*   Virgin? You called me a virgin?

ZORBÁ   But you are, my pigeon, you are my virgin.

HORTENSE   I, who have been loved by so many . . . I, a virgin?

ZORBÁ   Yes, my love, each new time, a virgin . . . with
each new one, a virgin. It is the wonder and mystery
and beauty of woman. Because with each new one, she
forgets the last one . . . See? Right now, you are blush-
ing, like a virgin, like a bride . . .

HORTENSE *(Wistfully)*   A bride? That I have never been.
Perhaps, as you say, many times a virgin . . . but a
bride, never.

ZORBÁ *(Slightly uneasy)*   Well, we can't have everything.

HORTENSE   It has always been my wish, my fondest wish.
(Dreaming) Someday to have a husband . . . a real
husband. Do you think it's possible, Zorbá?

ZORBÁ   Perhaps, my bouboulina . . . perhaps after you
take the youth treatment . . . *(Strokes her)* Meanwhile
rest, rest in my arms, my virgin . . .
   (The lights slowly fade)

SCENE 6

The scene is the entrance to the mine. Some of the men are seated on the ground and are eating. There are women (their wives) with them. The group includes MAVRODANI *and* PAVLI, *who are sitting together.* NIKOS *is seated at a table, checking off the names of the men. Two of them are standing in front of him. Some monks enter chanting. They cross to* NIKOS *as* ZORBÁ *enters from the mine.*

NIKOS Name?

GEORGI Georgi.
    (NIKOS *writes it down*)

NIKOS Next?
    (*The monks pick up the chant loudly*)

ZORBÁ Boss, give me a few coins.
    (NIKOS *does, and* ZORBÁ *hands them to the monks. They continue to chant for a few moments.* ZORBÁ *hands them a few more coins and they exit*)

NIKOS Your name?

KATAPOLIS Katapolis.

KONSTANDI When will we get paid?

NIKOS At the end of the week. Saturday . . .
    (*The man turns away and bumps into* MIMIKO, *who has just run in.* MIMIKO *jostles* MANOLAKAS, *who is seated on the ground*)

MANOLAKAS Watch where you're going. Go away. Go
home, fool!
(MIMIKO *cringes*)

NIKOS Just a minute. He works for me! (MIMIKO *smiles
proudly. To the next man*) Your name?

KONSTANDI Konstandi.

NIKOS *(To* ZORBÁ*)* You have nine men so far. Is that
enough?

ZORBÁ For right now, plenty.

NIKOS How does it look to you?

ZORBÁ It's neglected, it's falling apart. We'll need a lot of
new equipment. It'll cost money.

NIKOS And with the new equipment?

ZORBÁ *(Shrugs)* Who knows? If we can mine ten tons a
day, we might make out. If you want to try . . . it's up
to you.

NIKOS How much will it cost?

ZORBÁ It's not cheap . . . I don't know. It's up to you.

NIKOS *(Hesitates and looks around)* Get the equipment.
I want to stay here.

ZORBÁ Bravo, boss! A new life, eh?
(He grabs him warmly)

NIKOS Perhaps. *(Pulls away from the embrace uncom-
fortably)* How long will it take to get it?

ZORBÁ   A few days, anyway. I'll have to make a trip to
Khania . . . *(To the men)* Hurry up with that food. We
have to go through two shafts today.
   (He exits into the mine as the WIDOW *enters, carrying a jug and a paper bag. The ad-lib chatter stops
as the people stare at her)*

WIDOW   Mimiko, your lunch.

MANOLAKAS   Go home, woman. You're not wanted here.

WIDOW *(Disregards him)*   Your lunch, Mimiko.

MANOLAKAS   I said, go home.

GEORGI *(Moves toward her lustily and puts his hand on
her shoulder)*   I'll take you home.

WIDOW   Don't touch me!
   (She spits at him. PAVLI *starts toward her, and*
MAVRODANI *stops him)*

PAVLI   Let me just say a word to her.

MAVRODANI   Stay away from her. She has no use for you.
She has no use for anyone.

PAVLI   Papa . . .

MAVRODANI   Are you my son! Go home, woman!

WIDOW *(Disregards him)*   Take your lunch, Mimiko.

CHYRISTO *(A villager. Grabs the lunch)*   I'll give it to him
. . . *(Passes it to another man)* Give it to Mimiko . . .
   (They pass it from one to another, teasing MIMIKO
as he runs frantically after the bag)

MEN Here, Mimiko . . . Take it, Mimiko . . . Your lunch, Mimiko . . .

NIKOS I'll take it.
(The WIDOW watches helplessly. NIKOS steps forward, grabs the bag from one of the men and hands it to the WIDOW)

WIDOW *(Gives it to MIMIKO)* Here, Mimiko . . .

ZORBÁ *(Entering. He has a lunch bag)* Back to work! Back to work! All of you! I said everybody!
(The men start off. ZORBÁ now notices NIKOS and the WIDOW)

NIKOS *(To the WIDOW)* I'm sorry.

WIDOW Thank you . . .

ZORBÁ *(To the WIDOW)* Nikos. Mr. Boss, we call him. He's the boss.

WIDOW *(Glances at ZORBÁ, then at NIKOS)* Thank you.

NIKOS Your husband works here?

WIDOW I have no one here.

NIKOS Mimiko . . . is he a relative? *(She shakes her head)* You brought him his food.

WIDOW He is helpless . . . and kind . . .

NIKOS And he has no one here . . .

WIDOW   Yes. Thank you.
   (She starts to exit. NIKOS *watches her. She glances back at him as she leaves)*

ZORBÁ   Go after her.

NIKOS *(Startled)*   What?

ZORBÁ   The woman likes you. I can smell it in the air. Go after her.

NIKOS *(Annoyed)*   What are you talking about?

ZORBÁ   Go after her, boss. If a woman wants you . . .

NIKOS *(Irritated)*   Who says she wants me?

ZORBÁ   I do. If a woman wants you, boss, it's a great sin not to answer. God will wipe out all other sins. He'll have His sponge ready. But to leave a woman sighing, that sin He will not forgive.

NIKOS *(Angry)*   Stop talking nonsense. I don't grab at a woman. I am not an animal.

ZORBÁ   Yes, you are! If you don't know that, you know nothing! Boss, what are you afraid of?

NIKOS *(Defensively)*   I'm not afraid. I just don't want any trouble.

ZORBÁ   Boss, life *is* trouble. If I were as young as you, I would throw myself into everything. I would leap after that woman. I would fear neither God nor the devil. Boss, why can't you move?

NIKOS I can't change how I think, how I feel. Maybe sometime I'll be able, as you say, to move. But not too soon. Not too fast.
   (*The* LEADER *and the* CHORUS *appear*)

LEADER AND CHORUS
   Not too fast!
   Not too fast!
   Let it grow!
   Let it last!
   Nature knows when and why . . .
   (*They cross downstage, turning their backs on the audience and blocking most of the stage from view. The* WIDOW'S *room appears upstage of them, and the* CHORUS *breaks away, revealing* MIMIKO *and the* WIDOW)

MIMIKO The boss . . . he likes me.

WIDOW He does?

MIMIKO He likes you better. You like him, too? You like him, too?

WIDOW Get out, Mimiko! Out! Out!
   (*She shows him the door, and he runs off. She turns and is joined by* NIKOS, *the* LEADER *and the* CHORUS *in the song "The Butterfly." During the course of the number, the* CHORUS *turns its attention to* NIKOS, *who restlessly paces in front of his house, and then to the* WIDOW, *who opens a chest, removing a dress she wore earlier in her life. She holds it up before her*)

WIDOW AND LEADER
   Not too fast!
   Not too fast!

Let it grow!
Let it last!
Nature knows when and why . . .

LEADER *(Turning to* NIKOS) The butterfly . . .

NIKOS
I remember one morning
When I saw a cocoon in the bark of a tree,
I remember I marveled
That imprisoned inside
Was a butterfly . . . waiting to be free!

WIDOW AND LEADER
Not too fast!
Not too fast!
Let it grow!
Let it last!
Nature knows when and why . . .

LEADER *(To* NIKOS) Continue . . .

NIKOS
I was very impatient,
So I warmed the cocoon with the breath of my sighs;
And the butterfly trembled
And began to emerge
Like a miracle . . . right before my eyes!

WIDOW AND LEADER
Not too fast!
Not too fast!
Let it grow!
Let it last!
Nature knows when and why . . .

LEADER *(To* NIKOS) Sorry . . .

NIKOS

All at once I discovered
That his delicate wings were all crumpled and torn.
When he still wasn't ready,
I had made him be born.
I was stronger than nature
And I made him be born!
But the wonder of life has a definite plan,
So he died in my hand
By the will,
Not of god, but of man . . .

WIDOW

Not too fast!
Not too fast!

NIKOS

Every man has a moment,
And I'm waiting for mine, when I'm finally free.
But I mustn't be hurried.
Give me light, give me time
Like the butterfly.

LEADER

Like the butterfly.

NIKOS

Like the butterfly.

LEADER

Like the butterfly!

WIDOW, LEADER, CHORUS AND NIKOS

Not too fast!
Not too fast!
Let it grow!

Let it last!
Nature knows when and why . . .

LEADER AND NIKOS
Think about the story of the butterfly.
Think about the story of the butterfly.
Think about the story of the butterfly,
The butterfly!

WIDOW
Not too fast!

Blackout

SCENE 7

*It is the morning of the next day. The setting is the
exterior of* HORTENSE'S *inn.* ZORBÁ *is adjusting his knapsack as* NIKOS *enters.*

ZORBÁ   Well, boss, I'm off.

NIKOS *(Hands him some money)* Here's the money.
That's a great deal there. Try not to spend it all.

ZORBÁ   I've got to get a lot of stuff, boss—new cables,
pulleys, bearings.
    (MIMIKO *runs in*)

MIMIKO   Mr. Boss . . . Mr. Boss . . . *(Tugs at* NIKOS)
Mr. Boss . . .

NIKOS   Yes, what is it, Mimiko?

MIMIKO *(Hands him a bag of fruit)* The widow . . . she
sent these . . .

ZORBÁ   I'm not saying a word.

MIMIKO   She said to thank you.
    (NIKOS *looks at* ZORBÁ)

NIKOS *(To* MIMIKO) Tell her I thank her very much.

MIMIKO *(Surprised)* That's all? Nothing else?

NIKOS   No. Just thank her for the gifts.
   (MIMIKO *nods, then leaves*)

ZORBÁ   I'm not saying a word.

NIKOS   Good!

ZORBÁ *(Abruptly, indicating the fruit)* You going to eat
   that?

NIKOS   Yes. Why not?

ZORBÁ   Remember . . . you'll be munching on a woman's feelings, swallowing it, digesting it, and giving
   nothing back . . . The cork is too tight on your heart,
   boss. Let your feelings out.

HORTENSE *(From the rooftop of the inn)* Zorbá . . .
   Zorbá . . .

ZORBÁ   What?
   *(She steps forward and is now visible on the roof-
   top. She is carrying a bag of fruit)*

HORTENSE   Zorbá, I thought I had missed you. I thought
   you had gone.

ZORBÁ *(Weary patience)* You didn't miss me. I haven't
   gone.

HORTENSE   Here, I have something for you.
   (She exits)

ZORBÁ *(To NIKOS)* This is the day for gifts, eh, boss? I
   drive her crazy, the old goat.

HORTENSE *(Coming out of the house and giving him the bag)*   For your journey, my Canavaro.

ZORBÁ *(To* HORTENSE, *but aware of its effect on* NIKOS)   Thank you, my bouboulina. I shall eat this fruit tenderly. Each little bite will remind me of you . . . the apples of your delicate breasts . . . the plums of the plumpness of your cheeks . . . the pears of . . . of . . . I'll think of something.
    (ZORBÁ *and* HORTENSE *sing "Goodbye, Canavaro")*

HORTENSE
    Goodbye, Canavaro.

ZORBÁ
    Goodbye, bouboulina.

HORTENSE
    Don't forget me.

ZORBÁ
    I won't forget you.

HORTENSE
    Yes, you will.

ZORBÁ
    No, I won't.

HORTENSE
    Yes, you will.

ZORBÁ
    No, I won't.

HORTENSE
> Well, goodbye.
> Wait, Canavaro.

ZORBÁ
> What, bouboulina?

HORTENSE
> A kiss?

ZORBÁ
> Of course.
>> *(They kiss)*

HORTENSE
> Don't forget me.

ZORBÁ
> I won't forget you.

HORTENSE
> How long will you be gone?

ZORBÁ
> I'll only be gone three days.

HORTENSE
> That's time enough.

ZORBÁ
> For what?

HORTENSE
> To forget me.

ZORBÁ
> I won't forget you.

HORTENSE
 Are you sure?

ZORBÁ
 Yes, I'm sure.

HORTENSE
 Very sure?

ZORBÁ
 Very sure.

HORTENSE
 Well, we'll see . . .
 Wait, Canavaro.

ZORBÁ
 What now, bouboulina?

HORTENSE
 Will you bring me a present?

ZORBÁ
 Yes, I'll bring you a present.

HORTENSE
 You know, I'd like a ring.

ZORBÁ
 I know you would—I'll see.

HORTENSE
 No, you won't.

ZORBÁ
 Yes, I will.

HORTENSE
No, you won't.

ZORBÁ
Yes, I will.

HORTENSE
Well, goodbye . . .
Adieu, Canavaro.

ZORBÁ
Adieu, bouboulina.

HORTENSE
Don't forget me.

ZORBÁ
I won't forget you!
I promise I won't forget you!
I solemnly swear on my mother's grave,
I never, never, ever will forget you!
(He leaves. There is a brief pause, then HORTENSE
turns to NIKOS*)*

HORTENSE
He'll forget me!

NIKOS
No, he won't.

HORTENSE
Yes, he will.

NIKOS
No, he won't.

HORTENSE
　　Yes, he will.
　　I know it's true!

NIKOS　Why would he forget you?

HORTENSE
　　Oh, I don't know.
　　They always do . . .
　　But until they do . . . it's very nice . . .
　　　　(She exits into the house)

Blackout

SCENE 8

The scene opens on a blacked-out stage. The spotlight is on NIKOS, *who is seated on the apron of the stage, reading a letter.*

NIKOS *(Reading)* "Dear boss, I know I am some days late in returning, but let me explain what happened. When I arrived in Khania, it was dark and I wandered into a pleasant little café . . ." *(The stage lights up to reveal the interior of a café in Khania. It is a rather sordid place. A* BELLY DANCER *is performing in a desultory manner; she is chewing gum as she dances)* "There were some very charming ladies there, especially one . . . a lusty wench. Believe me, boss, when God put her together, He had His mind on His work . . ." *(The Belly Dance continues until the number is concluded. During the dance,* ZORBÁ *ostentatiously tosses money at the dancer)* "After a while, she noticed me . . ."
   (The dancer, placing his money in her costume, joins him at the table)

ZORBÁ   Waiter, a bottle of champagne!

NIKOS *(Reading)* "You know, boss, women love it when you spend money on them . . . Of course, I wish it was my money instead of yours . . ."
   (Another girl, noticing his lavishness, comes over to the table and sits)

GIRL   Don't bother with her. She's a bitch—a rotten little *bitch!*

ZORBÁ   I am not interested in her character.

BELLY DANCER   Get away, Athena.

GIRL   Shut up! I'm not talking to you.

BELLY DANCER   I said get away. I'll tear your hair out!

GIRL   I'll take care of you later.

ZORBÁ *(Pleasantly)*   Yes, you take care of her later. Right now, I'll take care of her. All right?

GIRL   All right, grandpapa . . .
   (She leaves them and returns to her table)

BELLY DANCER   Grandpapa! Did you hear what she called you?

ZORBÁ *(Annoyed)*   Grandpapa! I'll show her who's grandpapa! Waiter, give her a bottle of champagne! *(The action on stage freezes. To* NIKOS*)* I was mad, boss, not because of the insult, not at all. But the brazen thing had touched a sore nerve. Do you want to hear a story? Then, I'll tell you. *(He sings)*
   I used to have a grandmama who lived across the way
   From a pretty girl the boys would come to serenade each day.
   They would stand beneath her balcony, they'd whistle
   And they'd purr,
   And my grandma got to thinking they were serenading her.
   So she'd comb her hair and giggle through her few remaining teeth,

And she sat there throwing flowers to the fellows
  underneath.
In her faded red kimono she was awful, boss, a mess,
But she felt she was a schoolgirl in her first commu-
  nion dress.

NIKOS *(Reading)* "And then one day in anger I did a
terrible thing. I told her, 'Why do you rub walnut leaves
over your lips? I suppose you think they come to serenade you. It's the girl they're after. You're nothing but a
stinking old corpse . . .'"

ZORBÁ   That did it, boss. It broke her old heart. And with
her last breath, she cursed me: "May you suffer as I
have, Alexis. May you feel every gray hair. May your
bones creak and your strength fade with age." And that
woman's curse still scares me, boss. But I won't grow
old. Not yet, not yet . . .

NIKOS *(Reading)* "So with the help of your money, I
showed the little lady how frisky I am. We became quite
friendly; in fact she invited me to stay in her room. So
even if I spent some of your money on her, I did save on
rent. We went to the café every evening, till tonight,
when I said goodbye for the last time . . ."
    (The stage action continues)

BELLY DANCER *(To* ZORBÁ*)*   Get me some champagne,
please.

ZORBÁ   Sorry, it's all gone.

BELLY DANCER *(Rises)*   Gone? Georgi!
    (A man crosses to her and starts leading her off)

ZORBÁ   Him? Why him? He has no money, either.

BELLY DANCER   A young man with no money is better than an old man with no money. Goodbye, grandpapa . . .

ZORBÁ   Grandpapa! I'll show you who's grandpapa!
(The café disappears. ZORBÁ is alone on stage as the LEADER and the CHORUS enter. They sing "Grandpapa")

LEADER AND CHORUS
    Zorbá! Zorbá! Zorbá!
    (They make clicking and taunting sounds)

ZORBÁ   Listen, there are two Zorbás. The inner Zorbá is slender as a reed.

LEADER AND CHORUS
    Look at that! Look at that!
    Poor old man is weak and fat!

ZORBÁ   Thirty-two teeth!

LEADER AND CHORUS
    Look at that! There's no doubt.
    Every tooth is falling out.

ZORBÁ   And he wears a red carnation behind his ear.

LEADER AND CHORUS
    Look at that! Over there!
    Both his ears have long white hair,
    Ass's hair.

ZORBÁ   That's only the outside Zorbá!

LEADER AND CHORUS
    Look at that! Poor Zorbá.

Old and feeble grandpapa.
Weak and feeble grandpapa,
Weak and feeble grandpapa!
Grandpapa.
Grandpapa.
Grandpapa.
Grandpapa!
  (ZORBÁ *does the Grandpapa Dance. When he is finished, he exits, and* NIKOS *continues reading his letter*)

NIKOS *(Reading)* "So I'm coming back now. And don't worry—even though I spent a lot of your money, I did get some of the necessary stuff . . . All the best to the best of bosses, Zorbá."
  (NIKOS *folds the letter as* HORTENSE *enters*)

HORTENSE   That letter . . . it's from Zorbá?
  (She coughs)

NIKOS   Are you all right?

HORTENSE   I caught a chill. It's nothing. When is he coming back?

NIKOS   Soon, he says.

HORTENSE   Why did he stay so long?

NIKOS *(Wryly)*   He had his reasons.

HORTENSE   Does he . . . does he mention me?

NIKOS   What?

HORTENSE   Does he ask about me?

NIKOS *(Hesitates)*   Yes . . . He sends you his greetings.

HORTENSE *(Hurt)*   Greetings? That's all?

NIKOS   Well, his love. He sends you his love.
     (He starts putting the letter away)

HORTENSE *(Eagerly)*   That can't be all? So short?

NIKOS *(Pretending to read from the letter)*   Well, no . . .
"I think of her night and day."

HORTENSE   Yes? Yes?

NIKOS   "She is an angel . . . May our wings be united
very soon."

HORTENSE *(Laughs delightedly)*   Oh, he's so wicked,
that one.

NIKOS *(Bewildered)*   Wicked?

HORTENSE   Wings . . . that's what he calls feet, when
we're alone . . . the scoundrel. (NIKOS *folds the letter*)
Well, thank you, Mr. Nikos. Of course, I had hoped that
he might mention something else . . .

NIKOS   Something else?

HORTENSE   You know . . . he said something about a
ring, but . . .
     (She shrugs and starts off)

NIKOS *(Thinks, smiles)*   Wait! Wait, there is something
else. Of course, I don't know what it means . . .

HORTENSE *(Eagerly)*   What means?

NIKOS *(Pretends to read)* "I have a surprise for my bouboulina but don't even hint at it to her . . ." That's why I didn't read it before.

HORTENSE A surprise? You know what that means . . . He's made up his mind . . .

NIKOS *(Pleased with himself)* Well, I wouldn't . . .

HORTENSE Of course. What else? *(She hugs NIKOS in rapture)* Oh, Mr. Nikos, I'm so happy, so happy. I'm the happiest woman in the world!

NIKOS *(Uneasy)* You can't be sure, Madame Hortense.

HORTENSE What else could it be? What else? Ah, Mr. Nikos, to be loved again . . . not to be alone. Do you know what that means? To have someone . . . to open your heart freely. *(She sings "Only Love")*
Love,
Give me love,
Only love.
What else is there?

Two eyes, not seeing,
And two arms, not sharing,
And two lips, not feeling . . .
What good are they?

Doesn't the night seem endless?
Doesn't the day go slow?
Doesn't the dark look friendless?
And, oh, what good is that?

So
Give me love,

Only love.
That's everything.

Two eyes start seeing,
And two arms start sharing,
And two lips start knowing
How good it is

To feel . . . to touch . . . to care.

For after all,
After love,
What else is there?
(She exits slowly. The music changes, and the
LEADER *and the* CHORUS *approach* NIKOS. *They*
sing "The Bend of the Road")

LEADER AND CHORUS
Nikos! Nikos! Nikos! Nikos!
There's a girl at the bend of the road and she is wait-
ing for you,
Waiting for you.

There's a girl in a house at the bend of the road and
she is waiting for you,
Waiting for you.

There's a girl in a room in a house at the bend of the
road and she is waiting for you,
Waiting for you.

There's a girl on a bed!
There's a girl on a bed!
There's a girl on a bed!
In a room in a house at the bend of the road,
Waiting for you!

But the night is warm
And she needs no sheet.
So she kicks that sheet
To the bottom of the bed,
To the bottom of the bed,
In the lonely room
Of the house at the bend of the road.

Nikos!
She will call your name,
But when you won't come,
She will sit and cry
Like a little girl,
Like a little girl,
On the empty bed
In the lonely room
Of the big old house,
The house at the bend of the road.

There's a girl at the bend of the road and
      she is waiting for you,
Waiting for you.

There's a girl in a house at the bend of the road
      and she is waiting for you,
Waiting for you.

There's a girl in a room in a house at the bend
      of the road and she is waiting for you,
Waiting for you.

There's a girl on a bed!
There's a girl on a bed!
There's a girl on a bed!
      (The reprise of "Only Love" is played as the WID-
      OW's home appears. The CHORUS exits, but the
      LEADER remains, observing the following scene)

SCENE 9

It is dusk of the same day. Parts of both the interior and exterior of the WIDOW'S *home are visible.* NIKOS *enters, goes to the door of the house, hesitates, then knocks.*

WIDOW *(From the interior)*   Who is it? Who's there?

NIKOS   It's me . . . Nikos . . .

WIDOW *(Opens the door)*   You? *(A brief pause)* Come in. (NIKOS *enters the house, and the door closes behind him.* PAVLI *emerges from the shadows; he has evidently been watching the* WIDOW'S *house. He sees the* WIDOW *and* NIKOS *as they gently embrace; he utters a hurt cry and runs off. The* WIDOW *and* NIKOS *hold the embrace until the curtain falls)*

LEADER *(Sings)*
> For after all,
> After love,
> What else is there?

Curtain

ACT TWO

SCENE 1

The curtain rises on the village square. The CHORUS *is seated on chairs arranged in a semicircle in the center of the stage. Behind them, toward the rear of the stage, is the village church. The scene opens with the Bell Dance. It is interrupted by the abrasive sound of a mourning song, coming from within the church. The* PRIEST *and townspeople appear at the entrance of the church, at the top of the steps, and march down ceremoniously, carrying aloft the inert body of* PAVLI. *They are led by* MAVRODANI. *The* CHORUS *makes room for the procession as it slowly makes its way downstage. A woman in the procession screams and beats her chest as she exits.*

KONSTANDI What is it?

SOFIA *(A villager)* He's drowned himself.

KONSTANDI Who? Who drowned himself?

EFTERPI *(A villager)* Pavli. Mavrodani's son.

GEORGI A curse on the widow! She drove him to it.

SOFIA God make her pay for this.
　　(The procession exits downstage. The CHORUS *follows, leaving the village square empty)*

Blackout

Scene 2

The scene is the exterior of the cottage in HORTENSE'S *garden. It is early morning.* MIMIKO *is sweeping the steps in front of the house as* ZORBÁ *enters, carrying his valise.*

ZORBÁ *(To* MIMIKO*)* Getting ready for Easter, Mimiko?

MIMIKO Mr. Zorbá!

ZORBÁ *(Calls)* Boss . . . Boss, I'm back . . . Boss . . .

MIMIKO He's not home, Mr. Zorbá. He did not come home.

ZORBÁ *(Curious)* Not home? . . . Tell Madame Hortense I'm back. And coffee. Maybe there's some coffee, eh?

MIMIKO Yes, Mr. Zorbá.
  *(*NIKOS *enters as* MIMIKO *rushes off)*

NIKOS *(Coldly)* Delighted you took the trouble to return.

ZORBÁ *(Suddenly grabbing and hugging him)* Ah, boss, it's good to see you. I like you . . . I missed you.
  (Sniffs at him)

NIKOS *(Pulls away)* What is it? What are you doing?

ZORBÁ A woman's smell . . . *(Breaks into a grin)* You didn't sleep in your bed last night. Where did you sleep?

NIKOS   That doesn't concern you. What about the equipment? Did you get it?

ZORBÁ   Not all. Some. *(Sniffs at him appreciatively)* A woman's smell.

NIKOS   I said that doesn't concern you. *(Angry)* You wasted all my money on a girl!

ZORBÁ   Ah, boss, boss, I'm proud of you. It's the widow, no? Ah, fire and flesh in the right mixture.

NIKOS   But it was my money! It was for the mine!

ZORBÁ   I'm sorry about that, boss, honest. But man is weak, and I'm a man . . . And I'm going to make it up to you, every drachma. No salary till it's all paid up.

NIKOS   What about the equipment?

ZORBÁ   I got everything we need to start with. Later we can get the rest . . . We're still friends?

NIKOS   Why didn't you write to bouboulina?

ZORBÁ   Why? I have nothing to tell her . . . Don't worry. I'll give her a slap on the behind and she'll be fine.

NIKOS   I'm afraid she expects a little more from you.

ZORBÁ   Don't worry. I'll give her more! *(Brandishing packages)* See, I didn't forget her. I bought her presents.

NIKOS   Did you bring her the wedding wreaths?

ZORBÁ What?

NIKOS The wedding wreaths, and a ring!

ZORBÁ Boss, don't joke. I don't like such jokes.

NIKOS I told her that you wrote you wanted to marry her.

ZORBÁ *(Startled)* Why? Why did you say that?

NIKOS *(Mimicking* ZORBÁ*)* Man is weak, Zorbá, and I am a man. *(Mock regret)* I know. I created a terrible problem for you—unless, of course, you marry her. That would make everyone happy.

ZORBÁ Everyone? Who's the everyone? It would make her happy and me miserable. And the rest of the world wouldn't care. Who's the everyone?

NIKOS I know . . . It's terrible for you. What are you going to do about it?

ZORBÁ *(Concerned for a moment, then shrugs it off)* Ah, don't worry, boss. I'll manage her.

NIKOS But she expects you to marry her.

ZORBÁ Don't worry, boss. You worry about me too much. *(Sniffs him)* Mmm . . . you never smelled better. I'll take care of my woman and you take care of yours! (MIMIKO *enters with the coffee)* Oh, Mimiko. Well, where is she, the old tattered banner?

MIMIKO Madame is coming.
       (MIMIKO *exits)*

NIKOS Remember, Zorbá, she expects something of you. She's waiting for a proposal.

ZORBÁ She's grown old and fat waiting for a proposal. (HORTENSE *appears*) Ah, here she is, my beauty, my swan.

HORTENSE Zorbá!

ZORBÁ My bouboulina. I've hungered for a glimpse of you.

NIKOS Come, Madame Hortense.
        (Indicating the coffee)

HORTENSE No, thank you. I'm sorry. I don't feel well.

ZORBÁ What's the matter, my bouboulina?

HORTENSE I caught a cold.

ZORBÁ I've just the cure for you. A surprise.

HORTENSE *(Thrilled)* A surprise! (ZORBÁ *hands her a package with stockings. She is disappointed)* Is this the surprise? Very nice . . . Anything else?

ZORBÁ *(Hands her a package with a bow)* A beautiful bow to crown your lovely hair.

HORTENSE Very pretty . . . Anything else?

ZORBÁ *(Hands her a bar of soap wrapped in paper)* Here, smell!

HORTENSE *(Smells it through the wrapper)* Lovely . . . Anything else?

ZORBÁ *(Sweetly)* Let's not be a pig, my dove.

HORTENSE Thank you . . .
(She bursts into tears)

ZORBÁ What's the matter, bouboulina?

HORTENSE *(Turns on* ZORBÁ*)* Zorbá! What about what you promised in your letter? What happened to all those promises?
*(*ZORBÁ *looks at* NIKOS *accusingly)*

NIKOS Perhaps I should explain . . .

ZORBÁ No. *(To* HORTENSE*)* It's true I made certain promises in my letter, but when I wrote that letter, I was alone in a strange city. So naturally, out of my loneliness, I scribbled a few things . . .

HORTENSE What about, "I miss her night and day"? What about, "May our wings be united very soon"?

ZORBÁ *(Looks at* NIKOS *accusingly)* I wrote that? (NIKOS *nods. Aside to* NIKOS) That's too much, boss . . .

HORTENSE Then you didn't mean it, not a word? All those things about marriage?

ZORBÁ Of course I meant it, every word. Then. I swear to you, my angel, whenever I'm far away from you, I miss you very much.

HORTENSE And now?

ZORBÁ *(Innocently)* How can I miss you? You're here!
(He acts as if everything is settled)

HORTENSE   But you did want to marry me?

ZORBÁ   When I was in Khania, yes. Then.

HORTENSE   Very much?

ZORBÁ   Very much. Then.
    (He still believes everything is settled)

HORTENSE *(Sharply)*   Then why didn't you buy the marriage wreaths and the rings?

ZORBÁ *(Taken aback)*   What?

HORTENSE *(Sharply)*   If you missed me so much *then*, and wanted to marry me *then*, why didn't you buy the engagement rings *then*?

ZORBÁ *(Perplexed, thinking)*   Why didn't I buy the engagement rings . . .

HORTENSE *(Pressing him)*   Hah?

ZORBÁ   Hah?

HORTENSE   Hah?

ZORBÁ *(Gets an idea)*   I wrote to Athens for the rings. But it will take time. You know how slow they are in Athens. But the longer you wait, my bouboulina, the more beautiful you become.

HORTENSE   Zorbá . . .

ZORBÁ   What?

HORTENSE *(Pulls a handkerchief from her bodice)* I have something for you, too . . . *(She gives it to him. He feels it and shakes his head)* Open it! (ZORBÁ *opens it and holds up two rings)* The big ring belonged to Canavaro; he left it with me. The small one is mine.

ZORBÁ   I won't wear another man's ring. It's not decent.

HORTENSE   Only for a little while. Only until they send the others. *(Pleads)* Zorbá, Zorbá, here is a witness. God is watching us. Let's get engaged. Zorbá, my Zorbá!

ZORBÁ *(Looks at her for a long moment, then makes up his mind)*   Ah, why not? Right here under the sky, so God himself can see us. I'm going to make a toast. *(He takes a flask from his hip pocket)* My very dear bouboulina, my old comrade in arms . . . I've seen many figureheads in my day, nailed to the ship's prow, their breasts high, their cheeks and lips painted a fiery red . . . Today you are the figurehead of a great ship. And I am your haven. Strike your sails, my siren. You have reached port.
(He drinks)

HORTENSE *(Bewildered)*   What does all that mean?

ZORBÁ *(Irritated)*   It means we will be engaged.

HORTENSE *(Overcome)*   Engaged! Engaged! *(A slight pause)* And married?

ZORBÁ   Well, that's another thing. *(To* HORTENSE*)* Here, drink! *(To* NIKOS*)* Boss? *(He drinks)* Boss, you will be witness to our betrothal?

NIKOS   Nothing in the world would make me happier.

HORTENSE *(Overcome, she embraces* ZORBÁ)   Oh, Zorbá!

ZORBÁ *(Eases her away)* Please restrain yourself, my
   dear; it's Lent . . . *(Takes her arm)* Well, boss, do your
   stuff.

NIKOS   I'm not very experienced at this, but I'll do my
   best. For the servant of God, Alexis, and the servant of
   God, Hortense, now affianced to each other, we beg
   salvation, O Lord.
       (The LEADER *and the* CHORUS *enter. They join*
       NIKOS, ZORBÁ *and* HORTENSE *in the song "Y'as-
       sou")*

LEADER
   Dance, Isaia, dance,
   Isaia, Isaia.

CHORUS
   Y'assou, y'assou.

NIKOS
   A lily and a veil
   To represent her purity.

LEADER
   A lily and a veil to be sure.

CHORUS
   Ah, ah . . .

HORTENSE
   Did you hear that?
   Did you hear that?
   I'm pure.

CHORUS
   Y'assou, y'assou, y'assou, y'assou, y'assou.

NIKOS
> Some water from the well
> To summon back his innocence.

LEADER
> The chalice and the water just for you.

CHORUS
> Ah, ah . . .

HORTENSE
> Canavaro?

ZORBÁ
> What?

HORTENSE *(She splashes him with water)*
> You're my virgin, too!

CHORUS
> Y'assou, y'assou, y'assou.

NIKOS
> Wreaths of roses and cherries from the tree
> To show that she is married, she's absolutely married.

CHORUS
> She's positively married.

ZORBÁ
> She's certainly as married as she'll ever be.

CHORUS
> Y'assou, y'assou, y'assou, y'assou, y'assou.

ZORBÁ AND HORTENSE
> Confetti we can throw
> To represent our happiness.

CHORUS
    Ah, ah . . .

NIKOS
    Exchange the rings and drink the wine and then . . .

LEADER
    Dance, Isaia, dance,
    Isaia, Isaia.

NIKOS
    Promise you will never part again.

LEADER
    Dance, Isaia, dance,
    Isaia, Isaia.

NIKOS
    Canavaro?

ZORBÁ
    I promise.

NIKOS
    Bouboulina?

HORTENSE
    I promise.

CHORUS *(In a whisper)*
    Y'assou, y'assou, y'assou.

NIKOS
    Amen!

ZORBÁ AND HORTENSE
    Y'assou, y'assou, y'assou.

NIKOS
Amen!

ALL
Y'assou, y'assou, y'assou.

ZORBÁ, HORTENSE AND NIKOS
Amen!
(The three of them dance. When they are finished, the CHORUS *takes up the refrain)*

CHORUS
Y'assou, y'assou, y'assou, y'assou, y'assou,
Y'assou, y'assou, y'assou, y'assou, y'assou,
Y'assou, y'assou, y'assou, y'assou, y'assou.

ZORBÁ   Come, my sweet, let me give you the first respectable kiss you've ever had!
(They kiss)

CHORUS
Amen . . .

Blackout

SCENE 3

The stage lights up, revealing a road. NIKOS *and the* WIDOW *are walking together.*

NIKOS *(Talks haltingly)* What happened between us last night . . . you must not feel bad about it. Do you feel bad about it? *(She shakes her head)* Because I care for you very much . . . I want to know you better. I want you to know me better. I want to know everything about you, your life, your husband . . . You loved him very much? *(She nods)* Sometime you will tell me about him . . . I know that it is hard for you to say how you feel. You have lived alone so long. And all this anger against you here . . . Still, I do not think they are bad people—superstitious, crude, perhaps. The men see a beautiful woman living alone, they see how beautiful you are, and that is their foolish way of showing it, perhaps. But I do not think they are bad people . . .

WIDOW *(Sings)*
>Why can't I speak?
>Why won't the words come?
>Why do I stand here
>Trembling and silent?
>Why can't I speak?
>Why am I frightened?
>Why can't I answer
>What he is asking?
>Why can't I speak?
>Why am I waiting?
>Why don't I say it,
>Let out the feeling?

When we're together,
Why won't the words come?
Why can't I speak?

NIKOS   Excuse me for saying it, but it is wrong for you to
keep your feelings locked up inside yourself. I do not
mean that it is evil, but it is painful . . . And you must
not think you are so different that way. Many people
fear to let their feelings out freely. But you should try
not to fear . . . fear nothing, fear neither God nor the
devil . . . *(Stops, realizes he is echoing* ZORBÁ, *smiles
to himself, then continues)* Try to share your feelings
freely . . . share them with me . . .
    (A girl from the CHORUS *walks out in front and
    stands behind the* WIDOW. *They sing the duet
    "Why Can't I Speak")*

GIRL
Nikos, I want you.
Nikos, I'll say it.
Nikos, I feel that I'm living at last.
Nikos, I'll be good to you.
Nikos, I'll take care of you.
Nikos, my moments of silence have past.

WIDOW
Why can't I speak?
Why won't the words come?
Why do I stand here
Trembling and silent?
Why can't I speak?
Why am I frightened?
Why can't I answer
What he is asking?
Why can't I speak?
Why am I waiting?
Why don't I say it,

Let out the feeling?
When we're together,
Why won't the words come?
Why can't I speak?

GIRL
Nikos, I want you.
Nikos, I'll say it.
Nikos, I feel that I'm living at last.
Nikos, I'll be good to you.
Nikos, I'll take care of you.
Nikos, those moments of silence have past.

NIKOS   Someday I know we will be able to talk together . . .

WIDOW *(Sings)*
Why?
    (To NIKOS*)*
I will be late for the church!
    (She exits. He looks after her for a moment, then slowly exits in the opposite direction)

SCENE 4

The scene changes to the village square. ZORBÁ *and a group of villagers (including* MAVRODANI *and* MANOLAKAS) *are seated at tables in front of the café. Some people are entering the church.* ZORBÁ *is talking to the* PRIEST.

ZORBÁ I just want to be sure. When we officially open the mine Monday morning, you will give the benediction . . .

PRIEST Yes, yes, I will.

ZORBÁ But not just an ordinary blessing, Father. This is a rotten old mine; it needs a powerful blessing.

PRIEST I will do my best. Now, I must go . . . *(Starts out)* Why don't you come to church?

ZORBÁ Me? No, Father. You know the good Lord is everywhere, so why should I meet him in a dusty old building.
   *(*NIKOS *enters in time to overhear this speech. The* PRIEST *exits)*

NIKOS *(Amused)* Why do you say things to upset him?

ZORBÁ It's healthy for him . . . Keeps him alert! Boss, come have a drink.
   *(*NIKOS *and* ZORBÁ *exit into the café. The* WIDOW *enters. The villagers, who have been chatting quietly, notice her and fall silent. The* WIDOW *starts*

*toward the church. Everyone is watching her. As
she nears the entrance,* MAVRODANI *reaches the
door and bars her way)*

WIDOW   Please! Please! Let me go in!
(MAVRODANI *doesn't answer. She starts to move in
the opposite direction. The men seated outside the
café rise and block her way. She tries to get around
them, but they prevent her and force her away
from the café. Several women begin to shriek)*

WOMEN   Slut! . . . Murderess! . . . Kill her! . . . Kill
her!

WIDOW *(Appealing to them as she rushes about, hemmed
in)*   In Christ's name . . . In Christ's name . . . In
Christ's name . . .

MAVRODANI *(As several men approach the* WIDOW*)*
Stop! She's mine! *(The men retreat)* Manolakas! Avenge
your cousin!
(MANOLAKAS *advances toward the* WIDOW*)*

WIDOW *(Shrieks)*   Nikos! In Christ's name!
(NIKOS *exits from the café, holding a glass. He sees
what is happening and rushes toward* MANOLAKAS.
They wrestle, and MANOLAKAS *tosses him to the
ground. Two men seize* NIKOS *and hold him as he
struggles . . . The* WIDOW *retreats from* MANO-
LAKAS*)*

NIKOS *(Screams)*   Zorbá! Zorbá!
(As MANOLAKAS *approaches the* WIDOW, ZORBÁ
enters from the café. MANOLAKAS *raises his knife)*

MAVRODANI *(Crosses himself)*   I call upon God's justice!
(The WIDOW *has sunk to the ground)*

ZORBÁ *(Roars)* Lower your knife! *(All turn toward him as he rushes forward and faces* MANOLAKAS) Aren't you ashamed? A fine lot of men you are! A whole village to kill a single woman!

MAVRODANI Keep out of our business, Zorbá! . . . Manolakas, in the name of Christ, strike!
> (MANOLAKAS *leans over the* WIDOW *and raises his knife.* ZORBÁ *seizes his arm and they struggle . . . The* WIDOW *gets to her knees, tries to crawl away, but she is hemmed in . . . Several men seize* ZORBÁ, *trying to pull him away from* MANOLAKAS)

MANOLAKAS Keep away! Nobody's to come near. Keep away!
> *(The struggle continues.* MANOLAKAS *bites* ZORBÁ'S *ear . . . Suddenly* ZORBÁ *hits him in the stomach, and* MANOLAKAS *sinks to the ground.* ZORBÁ *grabs his knife and throws it away)*

ZORBÁ *(To the* WIDOW) Get up! Come with me!
> *(The* WIDOW *starts to rise. As she does,* MAVRODANI *rushes forward, knife upraised)*

MAVRODANI Widow!
> *(He stabs her. The crowd closes in. Upstage, in front of the church, a young sexton tolls the church bell. The* PRIEST *stands waiting. The* CROWD *looks up, slowly draws away from the body, walks up the steps to the church and enters it. The* WIDOW'S *body is revealed in the center of the stage,* NIKOS *kneeling over her)*

ZORBÁ *(In a choked voice)* Come, boss, let's get away.
> (NIKOS *does not move. The* CHORUS, *which has wit-*

nessed the whole scene on the periphery, turns to-
ward the church. Some members enter the church
and others gather at the foot of the steps. NIKOS *is*
still kneeling over the body of the WIDOW *as the*
lights fade into darkness)

SCENE 5

In the dark we hear a religious chant sung by monks. The scene has changed to the mine entrance. There is a large table with refreshments opposite the entrance. We see the PRIEST *upstage; the only light, a dim red one, comes from the incense holder he is swinging before him. The* SEXTON, ZORBÁ *and a crowd of villagers are only vaguely discernible in the light's reflection.*

SEXTON *(Sings)*
    We pray to God.

PRIEST   O Heavenly Father, in Thy everlasting goodness, look down upon us poor sinners . . .

SEXTON *(Sings)*
    We pray to God.

PRIEST   In the name of the Holy Trinity and Holy Virgin, Lord bless this mine.
    (The stage lights up. It is morning. All the villagers are gathered for the opening of the mine)

ZORBÁ   Amen!

CROWD   Amen.

PRIEST   And furthermore, O Lord—

ZORBÁ   Father, I'm sure the good Lord got the message. Let's not bore Him . . . God bless the mine! *(The vil-*

lagers begin to dance . . . NIKOS *enters)* Hey, boss,
have a drink . . .

NIKOS *(Angrily)* What's going on? Who arranged all
this?

ZORBÁ I did. For the opening of the mine. Mining is
heavy work, boss. We should start with a light heart.

NIKOS *(Outraged)* A light heart?

ZORBÁ It happened, boss. It's over. This is now . . .
Come, have a drink.

NIKOS *(A brief pause, then coldly)* I don't understand
you, Zorbá. I don't understand you at all.
    *(He exits. The villagers again begin their dance,
    joined by* ZORBÁ, *and when it is over, there is a
    general hubbub during which* NIKOS *re-enters.
    Some people take refreshments—wine, cheese,
    bread—from the table, while others peer into the
    mine entrance)*

FIVOS *(A villager)* How soon will we start to work?

CONSTABLE I don't know.

FIVOS Do you think this old mine can still be worked?

CONSTABLE I don't know.

FIVOS Will they use all of us or just a few today?

CONSTABLE *(Irritated)* I don't know. I don't know anything. Just because a man wears a uniform, that doesn't
mean he knows anything!

DESPO   When the crops failed, I prayed to the Blessed Virgin for a miracle, and she heard me.

GEORGI   The Blessed Virgin isn't opening the mine . . . he is.
    (He indicates NIKOS)

DESPO   Don't blaspheme, Georgi.

ZORBÁ   I feel good, boss. I feel very good.

NIKOS   I don't. When do you start work? Instead of wasting time with these people!

ZORBÁ   Right now, boss, right now. We'll have to dynamite one small section . . . loosen the earth; it's hard as steel. After that we can go in. *(Calls)* Listen! *(Picks up the dynamite and the fuse)* I need a man to go in with me . . . to take care of the fuse . . . *(Looks around among the men, then points to* MANOLAKAS, *who has been in the background)* You!

MANOLAKAS   I don't go with you!

ZORBÁ   I give the orders here. You do what I say!

MANOLAKAS *(In fury)*   You want to disgrace me again, ordering me around like a dog? You disgraced me once, in front of the whole village.

ZORBÁ   I didn't disgrace you. You fought well, I fought better.

MANOLAKAS   You fought better, an old man like you? I'm going to wipe out that disgrace right now. *(Pulls out a knife)* Fetch your knife, old man.

ZORBÁ   No knives. Put away your knife.
   (MANOLAKAS *does. They start toward each other.*
   The PRIEST *rushes between them*)

PRIEST   Stop! Manolakas! And you, Zorbá! Shame on you!

MANOLAKAS   He's dishonored me!

ZORBÁ   He chewed my ear!

PRIEST *(To* MANOLAKAS*)*   No one can dishonor you as
   easily as that. The whole village knows you're a brave
   man. What's happened is over and done with. Come,
   shake hands, both of you. (MANOLAKAS *hesitates)* Come,
   Zorbá. Let's have peace between you.

ZORBÁ *(Extends his hand)*   Here's my hand . . .

MANOLAKAS   Just to please you, Father . . .
   (He extends his hand. They shake hands forcefully,
   then more and more vigorously)

ZORBÁ   You've a strong grip . . .

MANOLAKAS   You've a good hand, too . . .
   (By this time, they are wrestling vigorously with
   their hands, about to fight. The PRIEST *hastily runs*
   in front of them, then around to the table to get a
   bottle and two glasses)

PRIEST *(Hastily pouring)*   Drink to each other . . .
   Good health, Manolakas. Good health, Zorbá . . .
   (Anxiously) Enough. Enough hand shaking!
   (They obey, and each one takes a glass)

MANOLAKAS *(Solemnly toasting)*   May my blood run like
   this wine if I ever again raise my hand against you.

ZORBÁ *(Raising his glass)* May my blood also run like this wine if I haven't already forgotten the way you chewed my ear! *(They drink, and the villagers shout their approval)* Now, you're coming with me?

MANOLAKAS I'm coming with you.

ZORBÁ Pick up this wire and fuse . . . I'll take the dynamite! *(To* NIKOS*)* We'll be a few minutes only.
(He enters the mine, followed by MANOLAKAS*)*

NIKOS *(To the others)* All those ready to work, give me your names . . .
(There is a rush to line up before him)

GEORGI Georgi. You took my name last time.

NIKOS I know. Next!

KATAPOLIS Katapolis . . .

KONSTANDI *(Pushing him aside)* I was ahead of him. Konstandi . . .

KATAPOLIS I was here first.
(An argument ensues)

NIKOS *(Sharply)* Quiet you two!
(He writes down their names. Suddenly there is the sound of an explosion. They all pause)

KATAPOLIS It's all right. They set off the dynamite.

NIKOS *(To the next man)* Your name?

VASILIS Vasilis . . .
(There is another blast, followed by a series of

crashes, similar to a small earthquake. Simultane-
ously, a woman screams. The PRIEST *backs away,*
inadvertently knocking a little child to the ground.
A woman grabs the child away)

CONSTABLE *(Barring the entrance to the mine)*   Don't go
in there.

NIKOS   Zorbá! Zorbá!

CONSTABLE   No one goes in there.

VASILIS   How many in there?

KATAPOLIS   Two.

NIKOS   Zorbá!
(There is a pause, then ZORBÁ *crawls out, followed*
by MANOLAKAS. *They are both filthy and dishev-*
eled)

ZORBÁ   The timber collapsed. It was weak, rotten. *(To*
the men) All right, go home everybody. Nothing there.

DESPO   Blessed Jesus. What do we do now?

PRIEST   God will provide, God will provide . . .

ZORBÁ   It's no good, boss. Nothing holds . . . I thought
maybe it had a little life in it, but no, it's dead, boss *(To*
the others) I said go home! It's finished! Go home. *(The*
people all start drifting off, leaving ZORBÁ *and* NIKOS)
I'm sorry, boss.

NIKOS   I'm sorry, too.

ZORBÁ   Are you angry, boss.

NIKOS   Angry? No, why should I be angry? You did what
   you could. The mine is dead. I will forget it. *(Turning on
   him bitterly)* How could you drink with him? How
   could you shake his hand?

ZORBÁ *(Bewildered)*   Manolakas? What did you want me
   to do?

NIKOS   The man is a killer.

ZORBÁ   Then maybe I should have killed him. And
   maybe his cousin would then kill me. And blood would
   flow . . . and souls would die . . . and others would
   weep as you weep. No, boss. I've had enough of killing.
   Enough.

NIKOS *(Bitterly)*   You shook his hand. You forgave him.

ZORBÁ *(Annoyed)*   No, I did not forgive him. It is not for
   me to forgive. I am Zorbá. I am not God. If he is to
   repent, it is in his insides, in his soul, in his spirit . . .
   where his God lives. There he must repent. A shake of
   the hand means nothing. Only that I understand a little.

NIKOS   Understand? What is there to understand?

ZORBÁ   He wanted revenge for the death of his cousin. It
   is not for me to judge him.

NIKOS *(Angry)*   Yes, it is! We must judge each other!

ZORBÁ   *Me* judge *him?* Me! I have done bad things, boss,
   many bad things. I have pillaged, I have raped, I have
   wiped out whole families, whole villages. Why? For my

country. Because they were Bulgars, because they were Turks. Is that a better cause than his?

NIKOS   Damn it, Zorbá, I'm talking about a murder. That was different. That was war.

ZORBÁ   *(Angrily)*   Damn it, boss, don't hide behind a lousy word. War. Revenge. It's death all the same.

NIKOS   I can't accept it.

ZORBÁ   Accept it. Do you want to hear a story?

NIKOS   No!

ZORBÁ   Then I'll tell you. When my little boy died, everyone cried, they screamed. Naturally. You know what I did? I danced. They thought I was mad, but if I hadn't danced, I would have gone mad. I had too much pain. It had to come out . . . So I danced when my son died, and then I accepted it. Don't you see, boss. Death's going to come; it's part of life. It'll come to you. Today, tomorrow. Someone shoots you and you're dead. Or you die in bed. It comes to all of us, every animal, every flower, every man.

NIKOS   I know that . . .

ZORBÁ   The only real death is the death you die every day by not living. Ah, boss, what a strange machine man is. You fill him with bread, wine, fish, radishes, and out of him comes laughing, crying, loving . . . *only* if his soul is free.

NIKOS   *(Attacking)*   Soul! You talk about soul. Where is your logic, Zorbá? You do not even believe in the existence of God!

ZORBÁ   Good! Then may God the nonexistent grant me this prayer! May he keep his handcuffs off my soul . . . and may he keep me ever alert, good and on fire!

NIKOS *(After a pause)*   I cared for her, Zorbá . . . very much.

ZORBÁ   That's good. That's not logic . . . that's your soul speaking.
    (MIMIKO *runs on*)

MIMIKO   Mr. Zorbá! Mr. Zorbá! Madame Hortense . . . she is very bad . . . she wants you . . .
    (They rush off)

Blackout

SCENE 6

Four men and the LEADER *of the* CHORUS, *covered in black shrouds, come forward out of the darkness of the stage. They sing "The Crow."*

MEN

> Keera kee kee kee, keera kee kee kee,
> Keera kee kee kee, keera kee kee kee.

LEADER

> Soon
> We'll see the crow
> Drop like a stone out of the skies.
>
> Then
> Someone in bed,
> Old and alone, closes her eyes.

MAN 1

> I want the gloves.

MAN 2

> I want the scarf.

MAN 3

> I want the spoons.

MAN 4

> I want the feathers.

LEADER

> Caw, caw.

MEN
>   Keera kee kee kee, keera kee kee kee,
>   Keera kee kee kee, keera kee kee kee.
>   *(The four men and the* LEADER *move to the side of
>   the stage as the lights go on. We see the interior of*
>   HORTENSE'S *bedroom. It is afternoon.* HORTENSE *is
>   in bed; she is very ill. Four old women are seated
>   about the room.* HORTENSE *groans)*

EFTERPI   She won't be long, poor sinner.

HORTENSE   Zorbá . . . Zorbá . . .

MARINA   Much he can do for her now.
>   *(She chuckles)*

HORTENSE *(Mumbling)* Zorbá . . . my Canavaro . . .
>   (KATAPOLIS *enters quietly)*

KATAPOLIS   They're coming to take inventory of the
dead woman's belongings.

DESPO   She'll be in God's hands soon enough.

KATAPOLIS   Was the doctor here?

MARINA   Here and gone. Nothing more he can do, he
says.

HORTENSE   Dear Jesus . . . Zorbá . . .

KATAPOLIS   Well, don't strip the whole place.

SOFIA   What good are they to her after she's gone?

DESPO   She has no one, no kin . . .

EFTERPI And we'll pray for her soul . . .

MARINA We'll do that . . . we'll pray for her . . .

DESPO Hurry up and die, my friend. So we can get a chance as well as the others.

HORTENSE *(Mumbles)* Zorbá . . . my Canavaro . . .
    (ZORBÁ *enters, pushing one of the women aside*)

ZORBÁ *(To the women)* Out! *(Turning to* HORTENSE) I'm here, bouboulina . . . I'm here. Don't be afraid.
    (NIKOS *enters and crosses over to* ZORBÁ)

NIKOS How is she? What's wrong with her?

ZORBÁ *(Simply)* Nothing's wrong with her. She's going to die.

HORTENSE Canavaro . . . my Canavaro . . .

ZORBÁ Your Canavaro is here . . . And the boss, he's here, too, to pay his respects.

NIKOS *(Approaches the bed)* Of course, I'm here, Madame Hortense, to wish you well . . . And you will be well, I'm sure . . .

ZORBÁ *(Aside, gently)* Don't lie to her, boss.

NIKOS You're right, of course. *(To* HORTENSE) I'm here, Madame Hortense, because I love you.

HORTENSE *(Weakly)* Such a gallant man.

ZORBÁ Of course he loves you, but not like me, eh, bouboulina?

HORTENSE *(Smiles weakly)*   You're so wicked . . .
  (She closes her eyes. MANOLAKAS *enters)*

KATAPOLIS   Madame, forgive us if sometimes we spoke a
  harsh word to you. We're only men, dear lady. May God
  hold you in His right hand.

NIKOS   Thank you, Katapolis.

MANOLAKAS *(Too loud, unsure of himself)*   God keep
  you. I, too, want to say God bless you.
    *(*ZORBÁ *looks at* NIKOS*)*

NIKOS *(A moment's hesitation)*   Thank you, Manolakas.
  *(*KATAPOLIS *and* MANOLAKAS *exit. The* LEADER
  *moves forward from the side of the stage and joins
  the four old women, the* CROWS, *in singing the
  reprise of "The Crow")*

CROWS
  Keera kee kee kee, keera kee kee kee,
  Keera kee kee kee, keera kee kee kee.

LEADER
  Soon
  We'll hear the crow
  Whistle a low, beckoning note.

  Then
  Someone will turn,
  Face to the wall, clutching her throat.
  Caw.

CROWS
  Caw.

DESPO
I want her watch!

MARINA
I want her shoes!

SOFIA
I want her gown!

EFTERPI
I want her ribbons!

CROWS
Caw, caw.
Keera kee kee kee, keera kee kee kee,
Keera kee kee kee, keera kee kee kee.

LEADER
Soon
We'll see the crow
Perch on the sill, stare at the door;

Then
Make of his wings shadows that spill
Over the floor.

Crow,
Come from the cloud,
Black as the shroud she's never worn.

Crow,
Crackle and cry,
What doesn't die.

CROWS
What doesn't die,
What doesn't die,

What doesn't die
Never was born.

Caw! Caw!
Keera kee kee kee, keera kee kee kee,
Keera kee kee kee, keera kee kee kee.

LEADER
Soon
We'll see the crow
Circle and dive, flutter and climb.

Then
Someone in bed,
Barely alive, knows it's the time.

CROWS
Caw!

LEADER
Look!

CROWS
Caw!

LEADER
Look!
*(At the end of the song, the music continues softly
in the background)*

DESPO She's gone . . . poor sinner.
(Other old women enter)

WOMEN She's gone . . . She's gone.
(They advance on HORTENSE. *She sees them and
rises with a scream, clutching* ZORBÁ)

ZORBÁ *(Shoving them away)* Shut your traps, you old magpies! Can't you see she's still with us. *(To* HORTENSE*)* It's all right my bouboulina; everything is all right, my swan.

> (HORTENSE *opens her eyes, smiles and puts her arm on* ZORBÁ'S. *He holds her cradled in his arms)*

HORTENSE Ah, Canavaro . . . how young I was . . . how beautiful, like a dove.
> *(The music fades out)*

ZORBÁ You are beautiful still, my dove . . . and young.

HORTENSE So young . . . My mother dressed me in a white organdy gown, and she said, "Ladies and Gentlemen, my beautiful daughter . . . it's her birthday . . . she's sixteen years old . . ." And my mother said, "You will dance through life. You will dance all through life . . ." *(As she speaks,* ZORBÁ, NIKOS *and the others freeze, and* HORTENSE *rises and walks downstage. When she is facing the audience, she is as she was as a girl—radiant, smiling. She sings "Happy Birthday")*
My mother says that little girls are made of sugar.
Happy birthday!

My mother says my life will be a wide, white ribbon.
Happy birthday!

And all my tomorrows
Are waiting in a line,
Shimmering, glimmering,
Soon to be mine!

My mother says she looks at me and she remembers.
Happy birthday!

She envies me the love I'm just about to see.

But she was yesterday
And I'm tomorrow.
Happy birthday to me!
    (She dances)
And all my tomorrows
Are waiting in a line,
Shimmering, glimmering,
Soon to be mine!

My mother says she looks at me and she remembers.
Happy birthday!

She envies me the love I'm just about to see.

But she was yesterday
And I'm tomorrow.
Happy birthday to me!
    (She returns to the bed)
Goodbye, Canavaro.

ZORBÁ *(Sings)*
Goodbye, bouboulina.

HORTENSE *(Sings)*
Don't forget me.
    *(She closes her eyes. ZORBÁ looks at her, takes her
    arm from his and folds her arms together)*

ZORBÁ *(Simply, almost roughly)* She's left us, boss.

NIKOS *(Brokenly)* May God rest her soul!
    *(The women start gathering her things like mag-
    pies as MIMIKO enters)*

DESPO Amen . . . God rest her soul.

MARINA   May angels carry her to heaven.

SOFIA   May her sins be forgiven. Amen.
(They are hastily pilfering like vultures, all the while continuing with their blessings. NIKOS *tries to stop them)*

NIKOS   Stop . . . Don't . . . Have you no respect for the dead? Don't . . . It's sacrilege.
(The women disregard him. As he grabs one, she pulls away and continues scavenging)

DESPO   That's mine!

MARINA   Give me that!

SOFIA   Don't rip it!

EFTERPI   Lord bless her!

SOFIA   God love her!

DESPO   Take your hands off it!

ZORBÁ *(Trying to help* NIKOS)   Stop it, you old magpies . . . Vultures, all of you. Get out, you pack of gypsies! It doesn't matter, boss; she is gone . . .
(They disregard him and continue to scavenge as they murmur their prayers. ZORBÁ *grabs a pair of* HORTENSE'S *shoes from one of the* CROWS *and hands them, as a gift, to* MIMIKO, *who ties them around his neck.* ZORBÁ *and* NIKOS *stand helpless as the women empty the room, cackling as they leave)*

MIMIKO *(Whispering to himself, then screaming, as he exits)*   Murderers! Murderers! Murderers!

(The two men are left alone with HORTENSE, *lying on the bare bed.* NIKOS *looks at* HORTENSE, *then at* ZORBÁ, *who leans against a wall, heartbroken. His back is to* NIKOS. *There is a long pause. Then* NIKOS *slowly and clumsily starts to dance. After a few moments* ZORBÁ *turns and watches him, then slowly joins him. The dance builds in momentum and intensity to its finale, when they collapse in relief. Two members of the* CHORUS *then enter and give* ZORBÁ *and* NIKOS *their luggage and coats, preparing them for the following scene)*

SCENE 7

It is some time later in the day, and ZORBÁ *and* NIKOS *are on the road leading out of the village.* ZORBÁ *is carrying his knapsack, and* NIKOS *his own luggage.*

ZORBÁ   Got everything, boss? All your books?

NIKOS   Got them all.

ZORBÁ   Buddha?

NIKOS   I take him wherever I go.

ZORBÁ   So you're going back to Athens . . .

NIKOS   Yes, for a while at least. Then, who knows. And you?

ZORBÁ *(Looks down at his feet)*   Wherever they're pointing . . . That way, I think . . .
    (He indicates the direction in which his feet are pointing)

NIKOS *(Impulsively)*   Zorbá . . .

ZORBÁ   What?

NIKOS   Perhaps I'll come with you.

ZORBÁ   You think so, boss?

NIKOS *(Hesitates)*   Well, first there are some things I have to settle in Athens, but after that—

ZORBÁ   No, you won't. You're tied to a long piece of
string. You come and go and think you're free, but you'll
never cut the string in two. You need a touch of folly to
do that—d'you see? Your head's a careful little shop-
keeper. It won't let you risk . . . everything.

NIKOS   And you?
      (ZORBÁ *sings "I Am Free"*)

ZORBÁ
      I have nothing,
      I want nothing.
      I am free.

      I need nothing,
      I owe nothing.
      I am free.

      If my feet say come this way,
      I probably would.
      But if they say go that way,
      That way is just as good.

      I ask nothing,
      I judge nothing.
      I am free.

      There's one Zorbá,
      And that Zorbá
      I must be.

      Heaven waits for other men,
      But not for me!
      I fear nothing,
      I hope for nothing.
      I am free.
            (*He goes over to* NIKOS)
      Hey, boss! Do you want to hear a story?

NIKOS Yes.
(There is a pause)

ZORBÁ *(Incredulous)* You do? *(Beaming)* Then I'll tell you. *(He sings)*
> One morning in Salonica, I never will forget,
> I was passing by the oldest man I think I ever met.
> He was kneeling in an orchard when he turned and smiled at me,
> And he said, "Come watch me, sonny, as I plant this almond tree."
>
> Well, I'll tell you, boss, that fellow he was over ninety-five,
> And I think he had a week or maybe two to stay alive.
> But he had to plant that almond tree and when I asked him why,
> He said, "I live every minute as if I would never die."

Think of that, boss? He lived as if he would never die. I live as if I would die any minute. *(He sings)*
> For that reason,
> Just that reason,
> I am free.
>
> I see somewhere,
> I go somewhere.
> I am free.
> Think of that whenever you remember me . . .
> I fear nothing,
> I hope for nothing.
> I am free.

NIKOS We'll meet again sometime. I'm sure of it.

ZORBÁ We'll see.

NIKOS And stay out of trouble.

ZORBÁ   Trouble? What trouble? Oh, you mean women.

NIKOS   Among other things . . .

ZORBÁ   You're right. I've had my share. Maybe too much.
I'll give them up . . . someday! And you, what'll you
be doing?

NIKOS   Oh, read, write, study . . . because it is what I
like to do.

ZORBÁ   Like before . . .

NIKOS   *(Half to himself)*   Not quite, I don't think. When I
work, I want to work well, and when I sleep, to sleep
well . . . and when I love a woman, I want to love her
well and forget all the rest while I'm doing it.

ZORBÁ   You're getting smart, boss . . . almost as smart
as me.

NIKOS   You will write and tell me where you are.

ZORBÁ   Of course.

NIKOS   My boat doesn't leave for an hour. I'll walk a ways
with you.

ZORBÁ   No. Let's do it quick, here and now, like men cut
short smoking or wine or a love affair . . . Come, embrace Zorbá . . .
        (ZORBÁ *holds out his arms.* NIKOS *slowly ap-
        proaches him, and they fall into a close embrace.
        The lights slowly fade)*

Scene 8

The stage lights up; the whole company is seated in a semicircle, bouzouki style, as in the first scene of Act One. ZORBÁ *and* NIKOS *take their seats. They all sing the reprise of "Life Is."*

LEADER
> Life is what you do while you're waiting to die.
> Life is how the time goes by . . .
>
> Having if you're lucky,
> Wanting if you're not;
> Looking for the ruby
> Underneath the rot;
> Hungry for the pilaf
> In someone else's pot.
> But that's the only choice you've got!

CHORUS
> Life is what you do.

LEADER AND TWO WOMEN
> Life is what you do.

CHORUS
> While you're waiting to die.

LEADER AND TWO WOMEN
  While you're waiting to die.

LEADER
  This is how the time goes by.

                    Curtain

About the Authors

JOSEPH STEIN (author) a native New Yorker, is the author of Broadway's long running musical, FIDDLER ON THE ROOF, which won him a Tony and Drama Critics' Circle Award. His other Broadway shows include the musicals PLAIN AND FANCY, MR. WONDERFUL, THE BODY BEAUTIFUL, IRENE, JUNO, TAKE ME ALONG, KING OF HEARTS, CARMELINA and the comedy hit ENTER LAUGHING. He wrote the screenplays for both ENTER LAUGHING and FIDDLER ON THE ROOF. His current projects are the play, BEFORE THE DAWN and the musical RAGS for which he is writing the book, with music by Charles Srouse and lyrics by Stephen Schwartz.

JOHN KANDER (composer) and FRED EBB (lyricist) first collaborated on the musical FLORA, THE RED MENACE. Their subsequent shows were CABARET, for which they won the Tony, THE HAPPY TIME, 70 GIRLS 70, CHICAGO, THE ACT and WOMAN OF THE YEAR. For films they wrote CABARET, NORMAN ROCKWELL: A Short Subject, LUCKY LADY, NEW YORK, NEW YORK, FUNNY LADY, and A MATTER OF TIME. Their television credits include LIZA (Liza Minnelli), GYPSY IN MY SOUL (Shirley Maclaine), GOLDIE AND LIZA TOGETHER (Goldie Hawn and Liza Minnelli) and BARYSHNIKOV ON BROADWAY. Their current project is the musical, THE RINK, with libretto by Terrence McNally.